BYWAY
EATERIES
of MINNESOTA

Acknowledgements

To Jerris, my wife, without whose support, companionship and discriminating council, this eatery guide would not have been completed.

Note from the Publisher

No restaurant has advertised nor paid in any way for inclusion in this book. The restaruants were chosen by the author for their food, atmosphere and cleanliness and because they are enjoyed by both locals and tourists alike. Most have local or regional reputations and some have achieved national notoriety. We think this guide will be indispensable to the traveler who treasures Minnesota, its communities and simply wonderful food and companionship.

Book and cover design and illustrations by Jonathan Norberg

All rights reserved.
Adventure Publications, Inc.
P.O. Box 269
Cambridge, MN 55008

Copyright © 2000 George Warner
ISBN 1-885061-80-3

Printed in U.S.A.

Contents

Preface

We can all cite a litany of loses due to social and economic changes. These include drive-in theatres, the family farm, smaller communities in general and various Mom & Pop vendors. But, to the delight of Minnesotans, the hometown cafes continue to both survive and succeed on a state-wide basis. The good fortune of these main street restaurants, amid the row upon row of fast food and chain restaurants, is perhaps less accidental than related to the state itself.

Minnesota's diversity attracts a wide range of people interested in sports, cultural events, nature, regional and local festivals, antiques, historic sites and all kinds of celebrations. Also, the communities continue to retain and even grow their small town American spirit and profile. And, our well surfaced and well traveled two-lane roadways support downtown preservation by leading to the heart of many villages.

But really, the most vital component to the prosperity of the hometown café is the people. The café entrepreneur, the regular for coffee and chatter, visitor enroute, or those for whom the community billboard is the local diner, all combine to produce the cafes' stability and growth. Without these integral elements, especially the hours and dedication of the loyal owner and waitstaff, these truly wonderful resources of nourishment to body and soul would give way to the pressure of hurried and superficial activity.

The aspiration to identify and gather Minnesota's unique, one-of-a-kind cafes into a guide initially appeared a relatively simple endeavor. In truth though the required effort exceeded expectations and the personal enjoyment received was more than ever anticipated.

Having found these wonderful restaurants to offer terrific food and the most interesting themes (pigs, cows, coins and even bicycles to mention a few), the idea to form them into a guide seemed a simple one. Also, in addition to the delightful social interaction (customer/waitstaff banter is common), I have a new appreciation for the phrase "acquired knowledge." Gathered wisdom now includes (among other subjects) hay, the stock market, fishing, history, the storm of "42" or the summer/winter of "___." More data perhaps than anyone really needs to know.

The fact is these are real people serving real food - and the welcome I received was genuine. I found the mix between "regular" and "tourist" to be invigorating and small threads of commonalities quickly led to as much conversation and mingling as desired.

Naturally, given the distinctive nature of each restaurant, the amount of social contact with the staff will vary. These cafes tend to be very busy places. That fact alone made research difficult - it's hard to interview the owner when she/he is "at the grill"!

These truly are unique enterprises and the care taken by these extraordinary preparers of nourishment is remarkable. Theirs is not the 8-5 workday, but rather a labor of love which is often 4 a.m. to 9 p.m. and perhaps 7 days a week. I know you will enjoy the results of their efforts as do the legions of their satified customers.

My only disappointment - I never did learn how to play cribbage.

Introduction

The Byway Eateries of Minnesota is a guide to Minnesota's unique, one-of-a kind restaurants.

Particular emphasis is given to identifying traditional "Main Street" cafes with strong community ties and foods which are home style in character emphasizing "from scratch cooking." The book also includes restaurants with a distinctive nature or historical significance whose character shares this spirit of individuality. All the entries are Minnesota's own - no chains or fast food allowed!

These cafes shy away from trendy food stuffs, offering meals of a home made taste and quality. Beginning with great breakfasts of huge cinnamon and caramel rolls, with basic egg, meat and 'cake combinations, the menus move to lunches and dinners of real mashed potatoes, roast pork, homemade soups, liver and onions, hand-pattied burgers, daily specials and of course, those wondeful fresh pies. These are simple foods artfully prepared and provided by a waitstaff devoted to customer satisfaction.

For the readers' convenience, the book is divided into six regional groupings: northeast, northwest, southwest, southeast, metro and greater metro. In turn, each city is listed alphabetically in its appropriate region with the restaurants' descriptions and maps to assist in finding it.

If you would like to make suggestions of other restaurants to include, or provide feedback on the ones we have included, please see the form at the back of the book.

If you need help in finding these cities, state maps are available from the Department of Tourism at 651-296-5029 or 1-800-675-3700.

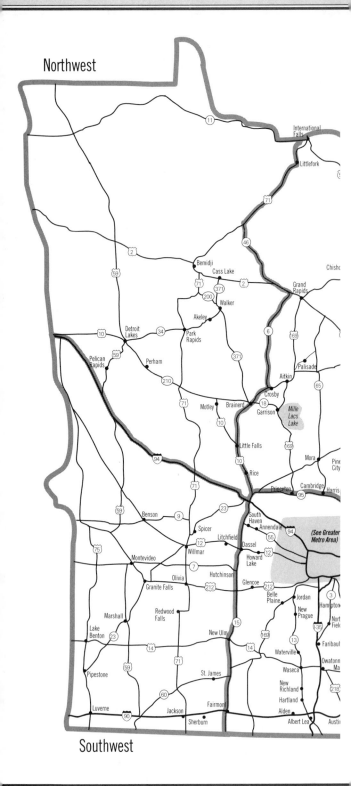

Northwest

Southwest

Geographical Overview

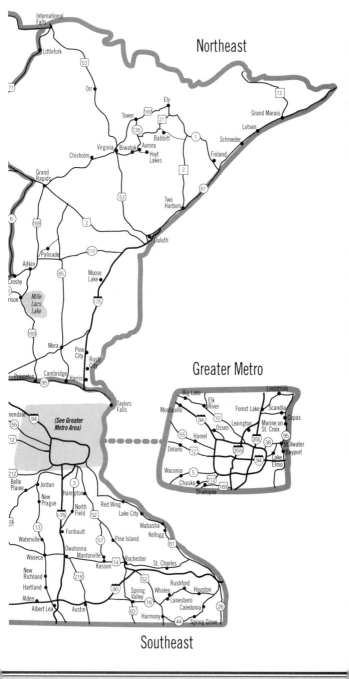

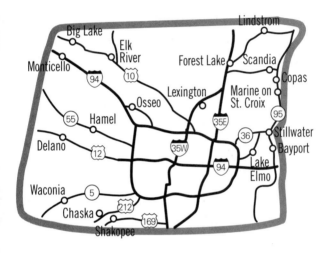

Greater Metro

BAYPORT

Bayport Cookery

The Bayport Cookery has received numerous awards for its cuisine, and is consistently reported as one of Minnesota's finest restaurants.

Dinners are served in an intimate and comfortable atmosphere which includes white linens and wine glasses.

The Cookery prepares a five course, fixed-price menu changing as fresh ingredients are available and new recipes introduced. Attention to detail is the standard.

Special dishes have included a Morel Festival and Garlic Harvest Dinner. (Those special five course dinners run in the $40 range.) The menu also reflects a seasonal theme.

*Special dishes have included a Morel
Festival and Garlic Harvest Dinner.*

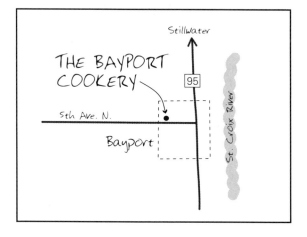

328 5th Ave. N., Bayport, MN 55003
Hours: One seating, 7 p.m. Wed - Sun
Reservations required
No children's menu
No smoking
Credit cards accepted
Phone: 651-430-1066

BIG LAKE

The Lake Cafe

The Lake Cafe

For over 30 years The Lake Cafe has provided home cooking for its loyal clientele of locals and tourists.

The city, on the shore of beautiful Big Lake, is located on Highway 10 just three miles north of Monticello.

Their cafe, with an interior reminiscent of a family room framed by beamed wood ceilings, serves meals that are big and tasty. Weekend specials include a Friday fish fry, steak on Saturday and walleye on Sunday. There is also a Sunday buffet from 11 a.m. to 8 p.m.

Their breakfast specials are featured Monday through Thursday, 5:30 a.m. to 11a.m., at hard-to-beat prices. Popular morning starters are the Cook's Hungry Man and Trucker's Specials with eggs, potatoes, meat choices and toast.

Service is friendly, prompt and very attentive to requests. A pot of coffee on the table keeps the cup filled and hot.

Popular morning starters are the Cook's Hungry Man and Trucker's Specials with eggs, potatoes, meat choices and toast.

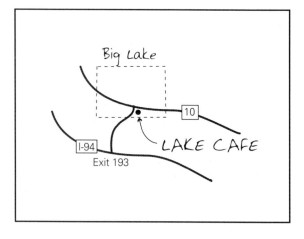

430 Jefferson Blvd. (Hwy 10), Big Lake, MN 55309

Hours: Mon - Fri 5:30 a.m. - 10 p.m.
        Sat - Sun 5 a.m. - 10 p.m.
        Closed Christmas
        (Call for other Holiday hours)

Breakfast served all day

Children's and seniors' menu

Smoking in designated area

Cash only

Phone: 612-263-2408

BURNSVILLE

(Jimmy's) Lemon Tree

With a little Greek bend to their home cooked foods the Lemon Tree serves up breakfast, lunch and dinner from their cafe located on busy Highway 13 near I-35W.

Set in a traditional configuration there is counter service up front with dining rooms along each side of the central kitchen.

Jimmy's 'all day' breakfast menu offers a nice collection of main courses with daily specials Monday through Friday. Specials vary on the weekends. The "Athenian" omelette with feta cheese, gyro meat and spices, or the Eggs Dimitri are two novel entrees which are included with Eggs n' Stuff, three egg omelettes and the Ranch breakfast.

The restaurant has three pages of luncheon items from salads (including a Greek Salad) to home-made soups, sandwiches, burgers and dinners. Among the Greek specialties are Greek-style pork chops and Souvlakia. Sandwiches with the Greek influence include a Pita Club, Gyro Pizza and a Greek Burger.

With an experienced waitstaff, service is friendly, efficient and attentive.

"Athenian" omelette with feta cheese, gyro meat and spices, or the Eggs Dimitri are two novel entrees.

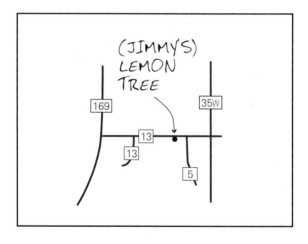

3511 W. Hwy 13, Burnsville, MN 55337

Hours: Mon - Sat 6 a.m. - 3 p.m.
        Sun 7:00 a.m. - 3 p.m.
        Open most Holidays

Breakfast all day

Children's and seniors' menu

Smoking in designated area

Credit cards accepted

Phone: 952-894-6700

C

CHASKA

BUTCH'S
RESTAURANT & TAVERN

Butch's Restaurant & Tavern

From its site in a 1876 brick building, Butch's conveys a feel of Old World character and charm.

The menu is a balance between the risk free assortment of burgers and the more upscale salad type sandwiches. All are served on fresh breads with tasty accompaniments. A nice selection of foods for visitors day-tripping the area. Dinners feature steaks, chops and chicken. A community fixture, their Friday Nite Fish Fry draws a crowd.

The popular restaurant is now owned by Kirk Swanson. Originally a general store, the structure was converted to a tavern named *Ein Deutsches Hans* or the German House.

The restaurant was added in 1962.

A golf shop with antiques adjoins the property.

A community fixture, their Friday Nite Fish Fry draws a crowd.

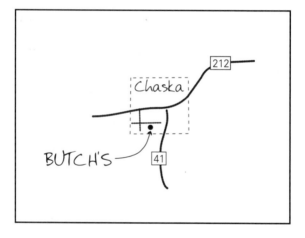

100 E. 2nd St., Chaska, MN 55318
Hours: Open daily 11:00 a.m. - 9 p.m.
Smoking in designated area
Credit cards accepted
Phone: 952-448-7400

CRYSTAL

EGGIE'S

Eggie's

One of Eggie's specialties is fresh homemade American fried potatoes – mounds and mounds of the best in the Twin Cities. Since 1976 this neighborhood cafe has served up 1,572,480 pounds of spuds, or as they state it 702 tons. Ordered with either onions, cheese or both this can become a meal in itself.

There are other reasons the regulars consistently line up at this exceptionally clean and neat cafe. Excellent service, a variety of quality foods and the patrons themselves account for Eggie's popularity.

Eggs (and of course American fries) can be ordered with Italian sausage or a homebaked Polish Kielbasa. House specialties include Eggs Ronaldo and a choice of traditional, country style, or "my way" eggs Benedict. There are 15 omelette choices ranging from the "El Paso," to Italian sausage with Provolone cheese, cream cheese, Kielbasa and cheese, or the Denver. Homebaked cinnamon rolls and muffins are made fresh daily. Buttermilk or blueberry pancakes and French toast round out the breakfast menu.

Elements of the lunch menu are daily specials, sandwiches and homemade chili or soup. The hot lunch specials consist of roast beef, meat loaf or chopped sirloin steak and a sandwich selection includes Italian sausage, chicken fillet, grilled turkey and burgers. Sandwiches are served with potato chips or can be ordered as plate specials with French fries.

Homebaked pies are the dessert feature.

*Fresh homemade American fried
potatoes – mounds and mounds of the
best in the Twin Cities.*

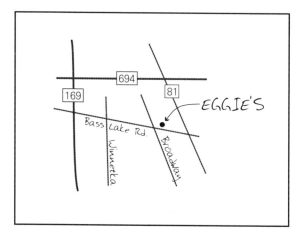

6418 Bass Lake Rd., Crystal, MN 55073
Hours: Mon - Sat 6 a.m. - 2 p.m.
            Sun 7 a.m. - 2 p.m.
Breakfast served all day
Children's menu
Smoking in designated area
Cash or check
Phone: 763-537-8719

DELANO

Edie Mae's Eatery

Set in a predominately country environment featuring woodcrafts and "tin," owner Edie Bren has been creating home-style foods in her sparkling little cafe since 1978.

Its attractive setting, across the street from the Crow River, affords the opportunity for a stroll after breakfast or lunch.

The menu's notoriety results from the usual and unusual. Breakfast on Texas style French toast with a batter of Edie's own creation, or a create your own omelette – literally. Simply ask and Edie will make it for you. Their American fries and hash browns have their own reputation owning to their "from scratch," homemade character.

Lunches include hand-pattied burgers (meat supplied from a local meat market), hot beef commercials (bread, meat, mashed potatoes, gravy) and a Hawaiian chicken salad with a sauce handed down from Edie's Grandmother. Homemade soups are also distinctive and notable including clam chowder and cheeseburger bacon.

The restaurant also opens for meeting and events upon request.

Lunch on a Hawaiian chicken salad with a sauce handed down from Edie's Grandmother.

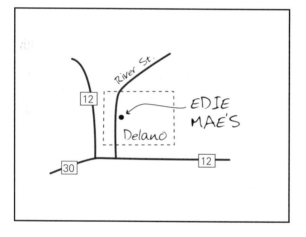

248 River St., Delano, MN 55328
Hours: Mon - Sun 5:30 a.m. - 1:30 p.m.
             Open Holidays
Breakfast served anytime
Children's menu
Smoking in designated area
No credit cards
Phone: 763-972-2919

ELK RIVER

The Olde Main
Eatery & Sweet Shoppe

The Olde Main
Eatery & Sweet Shoppe

The Olde Main Eatery, in downtown Elk River, is easily identified by its distinctive early 1900s appearance.

The cafe's catching theme is matched by a unique soup and sandwich menu which includes the Mile High Meatloaf Sandwich, the Stacker Hot Hoagie and the Chicago Classic $1/4$ pound frank. Salads are also a specialty, ordered with a choice of home-made distinctive bagel combinations, by name, the Top Hatter (bagel, egg and American cheese), Top Hatter with Tie (bagel, egg, American cheese and bacon – the "tie"). They also have a wonderful breakfast item called the Derby (English muffin with egg, ham and swiss cheese).

On the sweet side, owners Charlene and Margo create specialty desserts on a daily basis along with a chocolate brownie sundae and their "cheese-cake of the moment."

Unique soup and sandwich menu includes the Mile High Meatloaf Sandwich, the Stacker Hot Hoagie, the Chicago Classic 1/4 pound frank.

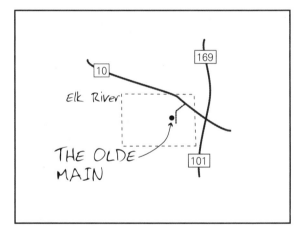

313 Jackson Ave., Elk River, MN 55330
Hours: Mon - Fri 6:30 a.m. - 4 p.m.
       Sat 8 a.m. - 6 p.m.
       Closed Sun and Holidays
Little kids menu
No smoking
Credit cards: V, MC
Phone: 763-241-8113

FOREST LAKE

Dona Le's Cafe

A stand out among hometown cafes, Dona Le's loyal customers gather routinely for morning games of cribbage, in-depth news analysis or Sunday, after church visits.

This is a family restaurant with owners Dona and Dale Schultz, and their three daughters and a daughter-in-law supporting them in the cafe's operation. They also like to define "family" as including their many loyal customers.

While participating in the cafe's light hearted banter is satisfying, the main attractions are simple dishes, finely prepared.

The "at home" feel of curtained windows and attractive plants are perfect surroundings for the home-style foods. Well known for their breakfast menu of the basics, these popular entrees give way to daily specials and hand-pattied burgers on homemade buns for lunch. The homemade soups, such as chicken dumpling or harvest, are popular midday selections.

The "at home" feel of curtained windows and attractive plants are perfect surroundings for the home-style foods.

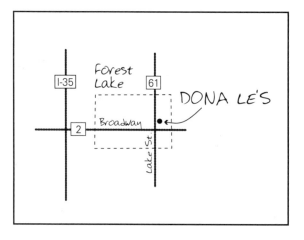

59 No. Lake St., Forest Lake, MN 55025

Hours: Mon - Sat 6:30 a.m. - 2 p.m.
        Sun 7 a.m. - 1 p.m. (Breakfast only)
        Closed: Easter, Thanksgiving, Christmas
        (Breakfast only on other major holidays)

Breakfast served all day
        (No pancakes after 11 a.m. Mon - Fri)

Children portions available upon request

Smoking in designated area

Cash or check

Phone: 651-464-7369

HAMEL

Countryside Cafe

According to his autographed picture on the wall, Mickey Rooney ate here twice in 1984. He came back for the same reason everyone else does – really wonderful food.

Since 1975 owner Peg Rasmussen has been preparing her quality home-style meals.

Using local markets as a resource, breakfasts begin with either wild rice or country sausage to complement the menus selection of eggs, pancakes, waffles and French toast. The homemade cinnamon rolls are a specialty of the house.

Lunches produce some seriously hearty homemade soups. The daily soup special might include a barley, chicken and dumpling, a very nice navy bean or a fresh mushroom soup. The Minnesota Burger, made with wild rice and garlic is a customer favorite.

On the dinner side, specials are rotated on a daily basis with such entrees as meat loaf or baked chicken served with real mashed potatoes and gravy. There are also "lighter" menu choices with some seasonal salad specials in summer.

The Minnesota Burger, made with wild rice and garlic is a customer favorite.

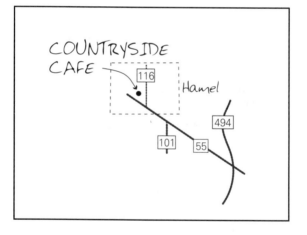

842 Hwy 55, Hamel, MN 55340
Hours: Mon - Sat 5:30 a.m. - 4 p.m.
          Sun 7:30 a.m. - 2 p.m.
Breakfast anytime
Children's menu
Smoking in designated area
No credit cards
Phone: 763-478-2101

L

LAKE ELMO

Gorman's Restaurant

Since 1980 Lake Elmo, which is slightly north and east of St. Paul, has been the home for Gorman's Restaurant.

The atmosphere primarily consists of a pictorial display of the history of the Lake Elmo area. Framing for several of the photographic displays are from doors at turn-of-the-century local buildings.

The menu features basic homemade breakfast, lunch and dinner items. Home-fried, skin-on potatoes are a wonderful breakfast accompaniment to eggs or their offering of eight omelette entrees. Their country breakfast, at an attractive price, is an everyday occurance.

Burgers and a comprehensive list of sandwiches make up the lunch menu which includes old-fashioned malts and shakes. Specialties of the house include a black Russian burger, or a sirloin steak sandwich. Fresh salads are popular as is the lite menu for alternative choices.

Dinner strays a bit for the conservative including interesting variations of the basics with a smothered chicken, pepper steak or teriyaki chicken.

Home-fried, skin-on potatoes are a wonderful breakfast accompaniment to eggs or their offering of eight omelette entrees.

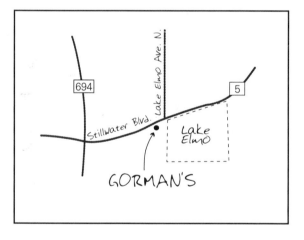

11011 Stillwater Blvd., Lake Elmo, MN 55042
    (3 miles east of 694 on Hwy. 5)

Hours: Mon - Sat 6 a.m. - 8 p.m.
         Sun 7 a.m. - 3 p.m.
         Open Holidays

Breakfast served anytime

A "Just for Kids" menu

No smoking

Credit cards: V, MC, D

Phone: 651-770-2476

LEXINGTON

Carol's
Calico
Kitchen

Carol's Calico Kitchen

For the last 11 years, the Calico Kitchen has been the harbor for a consistently expanding cadre of loyal customers.

The cafe's character is best revealed in a placard behind the register, "Live Well, Laugh Often, Love Much."

The visitor takes comfort in the friendly service, congenial co-patrons and the light country charm of the decor.

The food is homemade. Breads, soups, desserts, sweet rolls and salad toppings are all created in Carol's Kitchen. They also make their own jams and syrup.

Country cooking specials include Italian hash or a raisin-walnut pancake for breakfast. There are "Lo Cal" lunches and burgers served on homemade buns. Dinner choices include fresh roast turkey, southern fried chicken and the popular meat loaf, all served with real mashed potatoes.

Customers enjoy moving through the cafe to the adjacent shop and the opportunity to browse for nic-nacs and memoribilia.

Country cooking specials include Italian hash or a raisin-walnut pancake for breakfast.

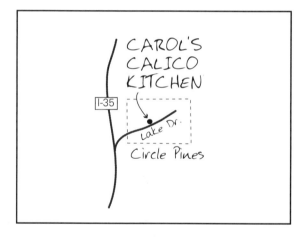

9100 N. Lake Dr., Lexington, MN 55014

Hours: Mon - Fri 5 a.m. - 9 p.m.
Sat 6 a.m. - 9 p.m.
Sun 7 a.m. - 1 p.m.

Breakfast served all day

Cash only in restaurant

Credit cards accepted in gift shop: V, MC, D

Phone: not available

LINDSTROM

Rainbow Cafe

Swedish immigrants settled this area in the 1800s moving west from their arrival in Taylors Falls. Of local interest, the city's lake side park exhibits a wonderful restored 1880 Swedish homesite.

This delightful heritage may account for the wholesome homemade foods prepared at the Rainbow Cafe. The restaurant's baker, a darling lady of 81 years, creates such pastry favorites as caramel and cinnamon rolls, coffee cakes and a lemon pie of statewide notoriety. Her special talents have been recognized twice by articles in the Twin Cities papers.

The Cafe is also an abode for casserole lovers. Daily specials of these filling and tempting dishes include hamburger-rice, tuna and tator tot. Additional entrees with a European flavor include Polish sausage and kraut, stuffed cabbage and homemade soups.

The breakfast menu presents a standard selection with the omelette varieties especially popular as evidenced by the 180 dozen eggs used every week. Eggs Benedict are a weekend specialty of the house.

The restaurant's baker, a darling lady of 81 years, creates such pastry favorites as caramel and cinnamon rolls, coffee cakes and a lemon pie of statewide notoriety.

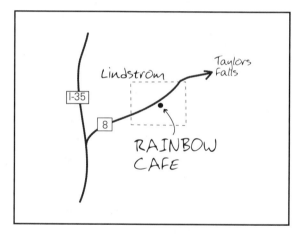

12715 Lake Blvd., (Hwy 8) Lindstrom, MN 55045

Hours: Mon - Sat 7 a.m. - 8 p.m.
           Sun 7 a.m. - 2 p.m.
           Open mornings on Holidays
           Closed Easter and Christmas

Children's menu

Smoking in designated area

Cash only

Phone: 651-257-5944

MARINE ON ST. CROIX

Voyageur Cafe

A unique cafe found in a unique and charming small town.

Supported by the "locals," the restaurant benefits from the weekend visits of loyal "city folk" and the ever present tourist.

Visitors are encouraged to not only sample the Voyageur's famous Anadama Bread but also learn of its interesting origin.

From their enjoyable menu of all homemade foods, the cafe serves breakfast and lunch. Menu selections include Hash-Plus, Jean Luc Toast and Loggers Potatoes for breakfast. A vegetarian meat loaf, Voyageur salads or a hearty homemade soup du jour are among the luncheon selections.

In terms of atmosphere, the theme is frogs which, as owner Anne Moore openly acknowledges, is an interest "gotten out of hand."

The restaurant is located directly across the street from the Village Park, site of the annual and wonderful one day spring art fair.

Visitors are encouraged to sample the Voyageur's famous Anadama Bread and also learn of its interesting origin.

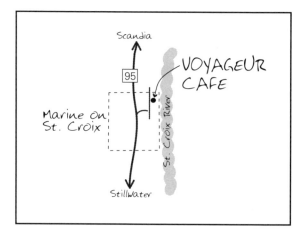

51 Judd St., Marine on St. Croix, MN 55047

Hours: Tues - Fri 6:30 a.m. - 2 p.m.
         Sat - Sun 8 a.m. - 2 p.m.
         Closed Mondays

Breakfast served anytime

Smoking permitted on outside deck

Cash only

Phone: 651-433-2366

MONTICELLO

Corner Cafe

Corner Cafe

Owner Rhonda Lagergren some four years ago brought her cooking skills from St. Cloud to begin this neighborhood cafe in Monticello.

Known for generous portions, an early morning hunger can easily be satisfied with a cup of coffee and the football size homemade cinnamon roll. Breakfast entrees including the list of Broadway greats are agreeably priced, complemented by "specialties" and "ol standbys."

The lunch assortment includes a nice selection of specialty sandwiches, sandwich combos, baskets, diet plates and either a soup-and-sandwich or soup-and-salad combo. As expected, soups are homemade with Rhonda's special chili available in season.

Fresh homemade pies are always a temptation.

Early morning hunger can be satisfied with a cup of coffee and football-sized homemade cinnamon roll.

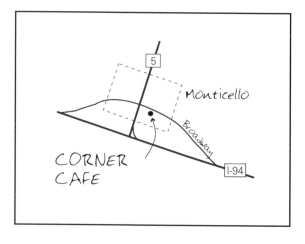

P.O. Box 116, Monticello, MN 55362
Hours: Mon - Sat 5:30 a.m. - 2 p.m.
       Sun 6 a.m. - 2 p.m.
       Closed Easter, Thanksgiving,
          Christmas Day
Breakfast served all day
Children's menu
Smoking in designated area
Credit cards: V, MC, D
Phone: 612-295-5100

MOUND

Scotty B's Restaurant

The definitive home-style cafe. It's no wonder they line up at Scotty B's – the food is tasty and plentiful.

Fortunately, for the last 10 years the residents of Mound, a touristy little hamlet on the north side of Lake Minnetonka, have been treated to the "fixins" from Scotty B's kitchen.

Omelettes, 'cakes and eggs supply the basic starters. Scotty's Favorite, a combination of hash browns, sauteed onions, green peppers and sausage, topped with a choice of eggs and either cheese or Hollandaise sauce, is hard to pass up. On down the menu, Hash and Eggs, the Hillbilly (eggs, sausage, biscuits and gravy), Country Fried Steak and Eggs, or the Croissant Scramble are tempting alternatives.

The menu picks up with an expansive luncheon selection that adds a taste of adventure. Sandwiches include a Monte Cristo, Giant Pork Tenderloin, Fajita Wrap and Turkey Broccoli Supreme to name a few. Soups and chili are homemade.

The Restaurant offers a nice selection of appetizers, a light fare soup and salad segment and a Veggin'out section provides meatless dishes. Dinners feature fish, chicken, oven-roasted turkey, a chicken stir fry and selected pasta entrees.

Along with Hot Fudge Brownies and ice cream sundaes, Scotty B's features fresh made pies supplied by a local bakery. Very, very tempting.

No wonder they line up at Scotty B's –
the food is tasty and plentiful.

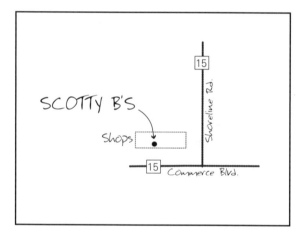

2244 A Commerce Blvd.*, Mound, MN 55364

Hours: Mon - Thurs 6:30 a.m. - 10 p.m.
          Fri 6:30 a.m. - 11 p.m.
          Sat 6:30 a.m. - 10 p.m.
          Sun 6:30 a.m. - 9 p.m.
          Closed major Holidays

Breakfast all day

Children's and seniors' menu

Smoking in designated area

Credit cards accepted

Phone: 612-472-5050

* Within the small strip mall

NEWPORT

North Pole Restaurant

A perfect short drive from the Twin Cities eastern suburbs leads to a wonderful little cafe called North Pole Restaurant. Founded in 1948 by Robert North and currently run by Robert's son Dave and Mary North. Still going strong, the cafe is spotless with great food and friendly and attentive service.

Breakfast dishes start with North Pole, Eye Opener, or pancake/French toast specials and a full selection of breakfast entrees. Lunch offerings include a nice array of sandwiches, homemade soups and chili, burgers and daily specials.

Dinners are ordered with salad, coleslaw or soup accompanied by a choice of potatoes and Texas toast. Liver and onions, roast beef, breaded veal cutlets, chicken and breaded cod are among the supper menu items.

For the sweet tooth, pies, specialty pies, sundaes, malts and shakes are on the dessert list. And for serious nostalgia, the root beer float is definitely recommended.

For serious nostalgia, the root beer float is definitely recommended.

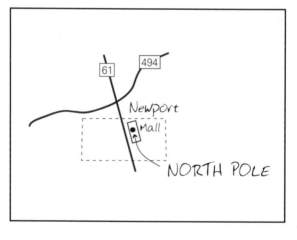

1644 Hastings Ave. (Hwy 61), Newport, MN 55055
Hours: Mon - Fri 5:45 a.m. - 7 p.m.
        Sat 6 a.m. - 2 p.m.
        Sun 7 a.m. - 2 p.m.
Children's and seniors' menu
Smoking in designated area
Credit cards
Phone: 651-459-9553

OSSEO

The Kopper Kettle Restaurant

Three good reasons to head for Osseo's downtown are breakfast, lunch and dinner at Tony and Rose Danato's Kopper Kettle.

The great thing about the meals is how home-style they are. Characteristic of their full breakfast menu, available to 11:30 a.m., are fresh homemade hash browns or fried potatoes. When ordered along side the Supper Kettle omelette topped with hollandaise sauce, the meal is complete. Eggs Benedict are another popular favorite.

Lunch may begin with a homemade soup (chicken rice receives a lot of call), followed by a burger or their special sandwiches including a hot meat loaf or roast beef.

The dinner luncheon choices also add an Italian flavor. Leading items are a veal and spaghetti combination or an Italian meatball hoagie. Among their best specials are a homemade Wednesday Spaghetti and a Thursday Lasagna.

Homemade fruit pies are a regular menu feature with a special homemade banana cream making an occasional appearance.

Homemade fruit pies are a regular menu feature with a special home-made banana cream making an occasional appearance.

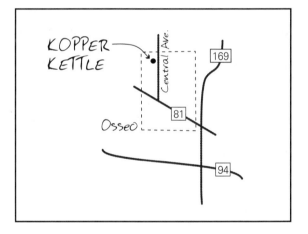

225 Central Ave., Osseo, MN 55369
Hours: Mon - Sat 5:30 a.m. - 8 p.m.
       Sun 6:30 a.m. - 3 p.m.
Full breakfast to 11:30 a.m.
     (limited breakfast anytime)
Children's menu
Smoking in designated area
Credit cards: V, MC
Phone: 763-423-6900

SCANDIA

Scandia Cafe

Scandia is the destination for breakfast or lunch with a touch of Swedish Heritage.

Meals are provided by the Scandia Cafe self-described as "Holly's Kitchen." The menu offers a wide selection for the diner.

Breakfast entrees include malted waffles, build-your-own-omelettes, a Hungry Man Breakfast and homemade muffins. Daily specials are served for lunch with appetizers, salads, burgers and a variety of "melts" and cold sandwiches. Homemade soups and chili are also available.

A decor theme of cows, cows, cows provides charm and character to the cafe's country theme.

Historically Scandia's attractions include the Gammelgarden Museum and Minnesota's oldest existing parsonage, the "Prast Hus."

A decor theme of cows, cows, cows provides charm and character to the cafe's country theme.

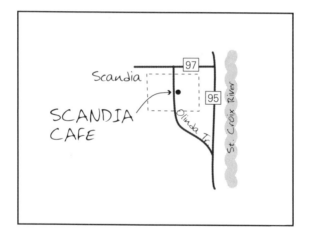

21079 Olinda Trail N., Scandia, MN 55073

Hours: Mon - Fri 6:30 a.m. - 2:30 p.m.
Sat 7 a.m. - 2 p.m.
Sun 8 a.m. - 2 p.m.
Closed major Holidays

Breakfast served to 11 a.m.

Children's menu

Smoking in designated area

Cash only

Phone: 651-433-4054

SHAKOPEE

Wampach's
Restaurant

SHAKOPEE, MINNESOTA

Wampach's Restaurant

Since 1954 Wampach's has been serving home-style foods to their legions of loyal customers.

With its area attractions, Shakopee hosts a large number of visitors and tourists who look to Wampach's as the choice for old-time favorites.

Their own invitation to "come as you are" fits with the casual atmosphere and the warm and friendly service.

Portions are abundant in satisfying breakfasts of hash, Chef's Morning Special or biscuits and gravy. Especially popular is their large platter of onion rings. The sandwich selections include melts, a Chief Shakopee, Dag Wamp, or $1/4$ and $1/2$ pound burgers. Soup of the day is homemade. Noon specials include meat loaf on Mondays and a wild rice hot dish on Tuesdays. Among the dinner entrees are liver and onions, ham steak, pork chops and walleye.

Homemade pies are a Wampach's specialty.

Their own invitation to "come as you are" fits with the casual atmosphere and the warm and friendly service.

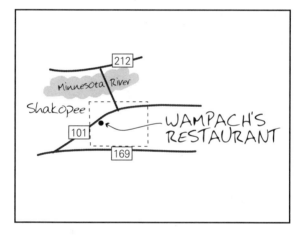

126-1st Ave. W., Shakopee, MN 55379
Hours: Mon - Sat 5:30 a.m. - 9 p.m.
         Sun 5:30 a.m. - 2 p.m.
         Closed Holidays
Breakfast all day
Children's menu
Smoking in designated area
No credit cards
Phone: 952-445-2721

SPRING PARK

**JOAN'S
LOG CABIN
CAFE**

Joan's Log Cabin Cafe

Lake Minnetonka's smallish community of Spring Park has been the home for Joan's Log Cabin for just about 20 years.

Truly a vintage "hash house," this diner serves great edibles in abundant portions at unbeatable prices. With an atmosphere of a 1940s road house, the crowds arrive for banter and food, each of which is served up by a wonderful staff including daughter Sandy.

For breakfast the fresh cinnamon rolls arrive dripping with icing. This is easily followed by a choice from their complete list of omelettes, eggs and meat, hash and eggs. A variety of specials and the taste tempting biscuits and gravy are served on Friday, Saturday, Sunday and Holidays. A must have are the just-like-Mom-used to-make American fries.

At lunch the menu features sandwiches and dinners. A challenge for the seriously hungry is the Texas Supreme – a $1/2$ pound hamburger, with three slices of cheese and two slices of bacon served with fries. Low-priced dinner selections include meat loaf, fish, salisbury steak, roast beef or liver and onions. These are served with a potato selection, home-baked bread and vegetable and a choice between soup, chili or a dinner salad.

The loyalists, whether off the yacht or row boat, young or old, trades or salesman, visitor or regular, all find Joan's a satisfying downhome cafe.

Truly a vintage "hash house," the diner serves great edibles in abundant portions at unbeatable prices.

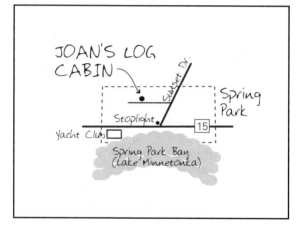

4136 Spring St., Spring Park, MN 55384
Hours: 6 a.m. - 2 a.m. everyday
          Closed Christmas Day
Breakfast served all day
Kiddie breakfast
Smoking in designated area
Cash or check
Phone: 612-471-7445

STILLWATER

Joseph's Restaurant

For over 25 years the green shingled cafe with its white spire has been satisfying hungry travelers from its hilltop location on Hwy 36, west of Stillwater.

Joseph's serves breakfast, lunch and dinner from a complete menu. Noteworthy French toast and buttermilk pancakes share in the breakfast selections of eggs and waffles. Midday decisions involve a nice selection of fresh salads (Joseph's Chicken Salad is outstanding as well as the new Mandarin Orange Salad), made-from-scratch homemade soups and plater style sandwiches. Joseph's Tower and Lumberjack are burgers for the major appetite. Suppers include steaks, chicken and walleye with a selection of lite entrees available.

The restaurant's specialty is their famous homemade pies created daily in the cafe's kitchen. Over 30 different selections are available. "Grandma's Favorites" include the award winning apple and a "Mary Lou's Rhubarb Delight." Pies are also available for take out.

With prompt attention and friendly service, Joseph's is an enjoyable wayside station with an unhurried pace.

The restaurant's specialty is their famous homemade pies created daily in the cafes kitchen. Over 30 different selections are available.

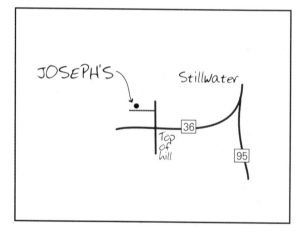

14608 N. 60th St., Stillwater, MN 55082

Hours: Mon - Thrus 6:30 a.m. - 11 p.m.
         Fri 6:30 a.m. - 12 midnight
         Sat 7 a.m. - 12 midnight
         Sun 8 a.m. - 11 p.m.
         Holidays 8 a.m. - 11 p.m.

Breakfast served all day

Children's menu

Smoking in designated area

Credit cards accepted

Phone: 651-439-3336

STILLWATER

The Main Cafe

The Main Cafe

As the name implies, this comfortable hometown cafe is located on Stillwater's Main Street, Highway 95.

Surrounded by the environment of historic Stillwater with its antique shops and art galleries, the The Main Cafe is a very popular casual eatery.

Beginning with their special Early Bird Breakfast, served from 6 - 10 a.m. Monday through Friday, the restaurant offers a variety of homemade foods. Start of the day includes the Gringo breakfast and Lumberjack potatoes, followed by luncheon salads and dinners of Cajun Chicken or a Meat Loaf Platter.

Friday and Saturday evenings, the cafe offers Greek specialties such as Gyros, Greek Salads, Taboule and Spinach Fillo.

The menu also provides Senior and Junior (10 and under) special entrees.

Their decor includes murals by a local artist and a selection of watercolor prints for purchase.

Friday and Saturday evenings the cafe offers Greek specialties such as Gyros, Greek Salads, Taboule and Spinach Fillo.

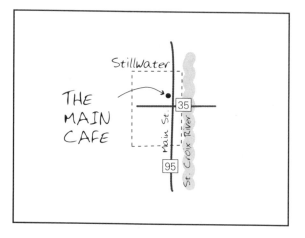

108 S. Main St., Stillwater, MN 55082

Hours: Mon - Fri 6 a.m. - 2:30 p.m.
Sat 7 a.m. - 3 p.m.
Closed Sun and Major Holidays

Breakfast served to 11 a.m.

Smoking in designated area

Cash, checks (in state with ID)

Phone: 651-430-2319

STILLWATER

River Oasis Cafe

Location, location, location. As a refuge for the Stillwater tourist, the River Oasis has a perfect site. That may be the reason there has been a restaurant at this spot for over 40 years.

Visitors mingle well with a crowd of regulars who return frequently to the home-style edibles the cafe prepares in generous fashion. The fare is not fancy, rather it is honest family style fixin's for folks who relish hearty meals.

Breakfast specials vary on a daily basis including, for example, eggs and Canadian bacon. Cinnamon and sticky caramel rolls are made fresh daily.

Lunch features their River Oasis Double Melt or BBQ burger platters with either a malt or shake served from the "tin."

Dinners offer a variety to satisfy most every taste with a menu that includes liver and onions, hot meat loaf sandwiches, or pasta and vegetarian dishes. Homemade soups and pies are always available.

Lunch features the River Oasis Double Melt or BBQ burger platters with a malt or shake served from the "tin."

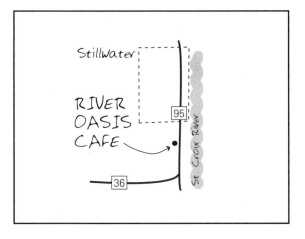

806 S. Main St., Stillwater, MN 55082

Hours: Varies to Season
        Summer: Mon - Sat 5:30 a.m. - 10 p.m.
        Sun 7 a.m. - 9 p.m.
        Open most Holidays except Christmas
        (Call for seasonal hours)

Breakfast served all day

Smoking in designated area

Cash only

Phone: 651-439-0928

W

WACONIA

Main Street Grille

Main Street Grille

Waconia, named for the bordering lake, is the site of the Main Street Grille which the Thorne family proudly calls their own. The town itself, almost a smallish fishing village, offers the charm of browsing through their interesting shops.

The Grille's menu is inclined to the "upbeat" with summer offerings of a fruited chicken salad with a raspberry vinaigrette dressing or their chicken salad on fresh homemade honey wheat bread. Always popular is the beef commercial (bread, meat, mashed potatoes, gravy) and the cafe's selection of 1/3 pound burgers are well known.

Breakfast decisions include a nice array of omelettes and the traditional eggs, meat and cake offerings, and dinners which include a baked meat loaf, chicken stir-fry or a seafood fettuccine.

The bright environment is a relaxed country atmosphere with a delicate bird house theme. Of special note is the attentive service and warm welcome received from this family operated cafe.

...summer offerings of a fruited chicken salad with a raspberry vinaigrette dressing or their chicken salad on fresh homemade honey wheat bread.

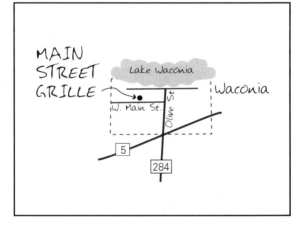

140 W. Main St., Waconia, MN 55387

Hours: Mon - Thurs 7 a.m. - 2 p.m.
        Fri - Sat 7 a.m. - 8 p.m.
        Sun 8 a.m. - 2 p.m.
        Call for Holiday hours

Breakfast served until 2 p.m.

Children's and seniors' menu

No smoking

Credit cards: V, MC

Phone: 952-442-5115

WAYZATA

Maggie's Restaurant

For the last 20 years Maggie's has brought a touch of Italy to the Wayzata Bay area, in addition to preparing a full selection of traditional American dishes.

The busy, busy restaurant draws a crowd and therefore a short wait (well worth it) is more common than not.

The flocks come to enjoy the breakfasts of eggs in all shapes and styles, a choice of 17 pancake, French toast and waffle entrees, or omlettes from Italy, Mexico and "Denver." One of the cafe's specialties is Maggie's French toast created from their homemade French bread.

Lunch and appetizers are served after 10 a.m. The sandwich board lists just about every conceivable meat and bread combo. Burgers, roast beef, grilled chicken, plus, plus, plus are among the choices.

Maggie's dinner selections are just as extensive. A bunch of American dinners, Maggie's or Gourmet Pizzas, Calzone, Baked Fettucini (either shrimp, alfredo, chicken, broccoli, or supreme) and of course Italian entrees are included.

Malts, shakes, hot fudge brownies and sundaes are the basic dessert choices.

Breakfasts of eggs in all shapes and styles, a choice of 17 pancake, French toast and waffle entrees, or omlettes from Italy, Mexico and "Denver."

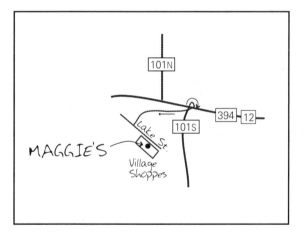

844 E. Lake St., Wayzata, MN 55391
(Village Shoppes Complex)

Hours: Mon - Fri 6 a.m. - 11 p.m.
Sat - Sun 7 a.m. - 11 p.m.
Closed Holidays

Breakfast all day

Kids Corner menu

Smoking in designated area

Credit cards accepted

Phone: 952-476-0840

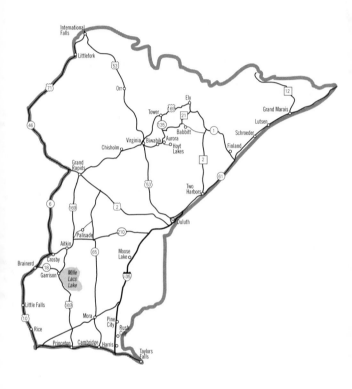

Northeast

AITKIN

Roadside Restaurant

This family cafe is a popular stop for traveler and native. Visitors to resorts and campgrounds of this prime outdoors area are attracted by the friendly staff and warm hospitality. With 30 years of service it's easy to understand the restaurant's following.

Their large menu has something for everyone. Beginning the day, some effort is required to pass the tempting case of fresh turnovers, muffins, caramel and cinnamon rolls. However, not to be missed are their great breakfast features with eggs Benedict at an unbeatable price.

Lunch ideas abound. Sandwiches - Reuben, steak, chicken royal or corned beef on rye are popular favorites. The Roadside's famous burgers can be ordered with varieties like sauerkraut and swiss, bleu cheese and bacon, or chili-cheese.

Roadside dinner features include a lite menu of salads, roast beef or petite burger and favorites such as liver steak, meat loaf and walleye.

For dessert, scratch pies are made fresh daily and that tempting case has a selection of six big cookies available.

Not to be missed are their great breakfast features with eggs Benedict at an unbeatable price.

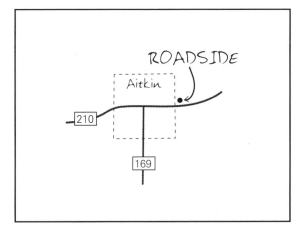

306-2nd St. N.E. Aitkin, MN 56431
Hours: Mon - Sun 6 a.m. - 10 p.m.
          Open Holidays
Breakfast served all day
Children's menu
Smoking in designated area
Cash and checks
Phone: 218-927-2113

AURORA

Megan's Family Restaurant

In addition to the fishing provided by area lakes, Aurora is home to a ranger station which has information on the hiking and bike trails of the nearby Superior National Forest.

Nearby are the Giants Ridge Ski Trails, both down-hill and cross country. In the summer, bike trails are available as well as a new golf course.

Megan's is the answer to satisfy the appetite raised by all these activities. Hearty breakfasts include a chili taco or Megan's own omelette. Chicken Philly, Beef Delux and burgers are available for lunch.

The dinner menu varies daily. During the week customers enjoy the 'stuffed hamburger steak', on Fridays a fish fry, Saturday prime rib or ribeye, and Sunday specials of turkey, chicken or BBQ ribs.

The home-style foods are served in a setting of Norman Rockwell pictures and homemade crafts.

Hearty breakfasts include a chili taco or Megan's own omelette.

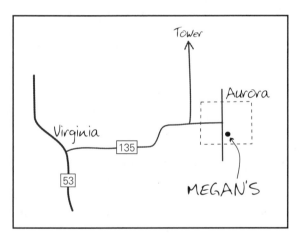

114 Main St. N., Aurora MN 55705

Hours: Mon - Fri 6 a.m. - 7 p.m.
 Sat - Sun 7 a.m. - 7 p.m.
 Closed afternoon of July 4, Thanksgiving,
 Christmas Eve and Christmas

Breakfast all day (except no hotcakes or French
 toast after 11 a.m.)

Children's menu

Smoking in designated area

Phone: 218-229-3418

BABBITT

Babbitt Diner

Thought has been given to rename this little cafe
The Babbitt Community Center. The Babbitt Diner
is the local source for all the "goings-on" whether
the topic is sports, politics or national events.
History is also a popular subject evoking furrowed
brows of concentration and serious reflections.

The foods are your basic edibles except co-owner
Robin Kroupa's desserts which result from her
bakery training. Innovative temptations have been
known to include chocolate cake layered with
chocolate cheese cake and a strawberry pie-cheese
cake combination.

Their well known and popular, biscuits and gravy
begins the day with additional choices of
omelettes, pancakes, Texas style French toast, and
homemade donuts, caramel and cinnamon rolls.
The lunchtime menu includes 35 sandwich choices
along with daily specials. Robin's chili (she
absolutely insists on making it herself) is a favorite
along with their homemade soups.

Dinners, available after 11 a.m., feature steaks,
chicken and cod, with alternatives of hot sandwiches and baskets. Sunday specials include roast
beef, pork or stuffed chicken breasts.

Robin's chili (she absolutely insists on making it herself) is a favorite along with their homemade soups.

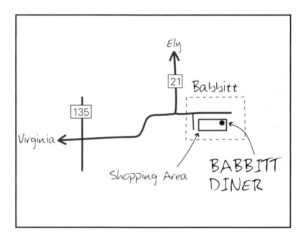

9 Commerce Rd., Babbitt, MN 55706
Hours: Winter: Mon - Sat 6:30 a.m. - 7 p.m.
               Sun 7 a.m. - 2 p.m.
              Summer: Mon - Sat 6:30 a.m. - 8 p.m.
               Sun 7 a.m. - 2 p.m.
              Open Holidays until 2 p.m.
              Closed Christmas Day and New Year's Day
Breakfast served all day
Will prepare children's meals
Smoking in designated area
Cash only
Phone: 218-827-3470

BIWABIK

Alden's Restaurant

Capturing the theme of its proximity to the Giants Ridge Ski and Golf complex, Biwabik has artfully transformed itself into a Bavarian hamlet. Alden's is located in the middle of this sparkling and interesting village.

Set in an atmosphere of northwoods pine, the cafe features an extensive selection of steaks, walleye and Italian entrees. Foods are prepared under the direction of owner Alden Rhode who served as chef for some of the Twin Cities finer dining establishments prior to relocating to enjoy Minnesota's northwoods attractions. Sunday dinners include homemade mashed potatoes with either roast beef, chicken or pork.

In addition to homemade caramel rolls, breakfasts include the usual complement of eggs, meats and 'cakes.

Luncheon items include homemade soups and pies and a choice of nine different melt sandwiches.

Owner Alden Rhode served as chef for some of the Twin Cities finer dining establishments prior to relocating to Minnesota's northwoods attractions.

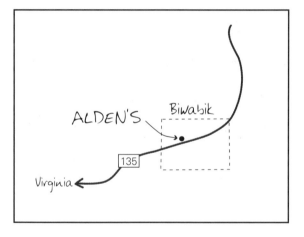

209 ½ W. Main St., Biwabik, MN 55708

Hours: Mon - Thurs 7 a.m. - 9 p.m.
        Fri - Sat 7 a.m. - 10 p.m.
        Sun 7 a.m. - 7 p.m.
        Open most Holidays

Breakfast served until 4 p.m.

Children's menu

Smoking in designated area

Credit cards: V, MC, D

Phone: 218-865-6371

BRAINERD (BAXTER)

371 Diner

Adjacent to Highway 371 North in Baxter, the diner is named for its location.

With period music in the background, the diner is distinctively 50s with signs and news clippings adding to the theme.

Making your food choices requires a study of the interesting menu. Examples of selections include the "56 Studebaker" and "64 Stingray" (burgers); "The Fonz" and "The James Dean" (chicken sandwiches); and the "Leader of the Pack" and "Alien Invasion" (breakfast entrees).

Breakfast is available anytime and the diner offers a Little Rascals menu for lunch or dinner and Little Go-Kart Racer breakfast selections.

Selections include "56 Studebaker," "64 Stingray," "The Fonz," "The James Dean," "Leader of the Pack" and "Alien Invasion."

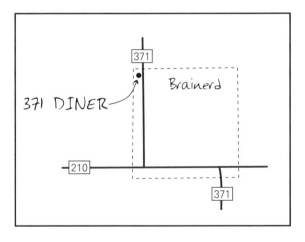

1175 Edgewood Dr. N. (& 371), Baxter, MN 56425
Hours: Summer: Sun - Thurs 6 a.m. - 12 midnight
             Fri - Sat 6 a.m. - 2 a.m.
         Winter: Mon - Thurs 6 a.m. - 12 midnight
             Sun - 6 a.m. - 10 p.m.
             Fri - Sat 6 a.m. - 12 midnight
Breakfast menu is provided
A "Little Rascals" lunch and "Little Go-Kart Racer"
Smoking in designated area
Credit cards: V, MC, D, AE
Phone: 218-829-3356

BRAINERD

MOREY'S
MARKET & GRILLE

Morey's Market & Grille

Morey's is a Minnesota legend serving residents since 1937. Their Brainerd location has been in existence for 20 years.

Morey's Market & Grille is a supplier of fish and seafood in a gourmet setting, with a unique approach to cafe ambiance.

The Grille's novelty is to have the dining area wander throughout the market. Character and interest are achieved by the seating of customers among counters of kitchen giftware and various provisions.

Naturally, foods are seafood oriented. This is the home of pan-fried walleye, and fish specialties dominate the menu. Homemade soups and non-seafood items are available, with an emphasis on freshness and interesting preparations.

*The Grille's novelty is to have
the dining area wander throughout
the market.*

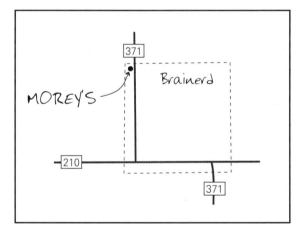

1650 Hwy 371 N., Brainerd, MN 56401
Hours: Grille 11 a.m. - 8 p.m. daily
       Market 8 a.m. - 8 p.m. daily
Children's menu
Credit cards accepted
Phone: 218-829-8248

CAMBRIDGE

Herman's Bakery, Coffee Shop & Deli

Herman's, a popular meeting and melting pot, has provided quality food and service for over 20 years. By reputation it has become a favorite stop for friends, family and travelers.

Food and beverages, purchased at the service counter, are carried to their eating area with seating available for 62 customers. Decor consists of a collection of Paul Detlefsen prints, with antique coffee pots and cookie jars rotated with seasonal decorations.

A daily variety of made-from-scratch baked goods is available with such not forgotten specialties as famous Apple Fritters and gooey caramel and large cinnamon rolls. Sandwiches, soups, sloppy joes, salads and meat pasties are all favorites for lunch.

A daily variety of made-from-scratch baked goods is available with such not forgotten specialties as famous Apple Fritters and gooey caramel and large cinnamon rolls.

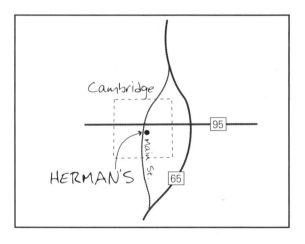

130 S. Main St., Cambridge, MN 55008
Hours: Mon - Fri 6 a.m. - 6 p.m.
        Sat 6 a.m. - 3 p.m.
        Closed Sundays and Holidays
Smoking in designated area
Credit cards: V, MC, D, AE
Phone: 763-689-1515

CAMBRIDGE

People's Cafe

People's Cafe

People's Cafe, with the unmistakable feel of a village cafe, provides travelers with a friendly dining experience. Owners, David and Cindy Stilson, continue the tradition of quality and service built on the 30+ year history of the restaurant. David has been associated with the cafe for 27 years.

The *Minneapolis Star and Tribune* has recommended the cafe's buttermilk pancakes and the folks in Cambridge give People's their best award for coffee, service and pies (made fresh daily).

The menu is proverbial. In addition to the huge fluffy pancakes, there are breakfast choices for every appetite (served all day), a nice array of burgers and sandwiches for lunch and, of course, those homemade dinners. No one really leaves People's Cafe feeling hungry.

The folks in Cambridge give People's their best award for coffee, service and pies (made fresh daily).

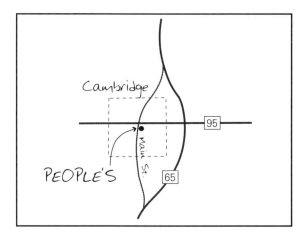

118 S. Main St., Cambridge, MN 55008

Hours: Mon - Thurs 5 a.m. - 8 p.m.
       Fri - Sat 5 a.m. - 9 p.m.
       Sun 6 a.m. - 8 p.m.
       Closed Thanksgiving, Christmas and
          New Year's

Children's menu

Smoking in designated area

No credit cards

Phone: 763-689-3198

CHISHOLM

Helen's Diner

Helen's Diner is located on Chisholm's main street adjacent to Highway 169. The city of Chisholm is home to the Ironworld Discovery Center which describes the heritage of the immigrants who came to work in the mines of Minnesota's Iron range.

For those with an interest in antique automobiles, Chisholm also has a museum of classic cars.

For visitors in the area, Helen's Diner is the place for wonderful hometown friendly service and homemade foods. For breakfast the daily Rise and Shine special is especially popular, and the luncheon sandwich menu is extensive. Monday to Friday the homemade chili is always available.

During the Holidays, the cafe is decorated with ceramics which Helen creates in her "spare" time.

For visitors in the area Helen's Diner is the place for wonderful hometown friendly service and homemade foods.

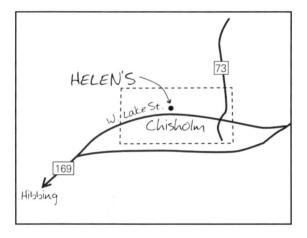

12 W. Lake St., Chisholm, MN 55719
Hours: Mon - Fri 6 a.m. - 3 p.m.
　　　　 Sat - Sun 6 a.m. - 1:30 p.m.
Breakfast served anytime
Smoking in designated area
Cash only
Phone: 218-254-7444

CLOQUET

Family Tradition Restaurant

Homemade heaven. Owner John Johnson has converted this former root beer stand into one of the areas best restaurants. Breakfast selections include the "must have" Family Tradition Muffin – one very serious treat. The kitchen also conceives eight different breakfast combinations including the #4, two eggs on hash browns served on an English mufffin, topped with cheese, or the Breakfast In a Hurry (scrambled egg, bacon and cheese) sandwich on a toasted bun. From 6 a.m. to noon the cafe features a daily breakfast special – this includes weekends.

Having served over 1700 in one day, the Family Tradition's secret recipe Coney Island hot dog, is the lunchtime anchor. However, this is certainly not the end of their menu. Burgers (Hot Pepper Cheeseburger for one), sandwiches (BBQ Chicken, Shrimp, Fish), dinners (Hot Turkey, Meat Loaf) or lite appetite selections are also available. The restaurant has also created a legend with its Pasta Chicken Salad served with a homemade bran mufffin.

Dinners with real mashed potatoes, roast turkey, meat loaf, walleye (and walleye fingers), shrimp, ribeyes and beef liver are alternative ideas. The cafe also has daily specials such as Goulash Wednesdays and Meat Loaf Mondays.

The clean little restaurant is nicely divided into counter and dining room areas with the friendly staff responding to the needs of the legions of diners. No wonder it's so popular.

Breakfast selections include the "must have" Family Tradition Muffin – one very serious treat.

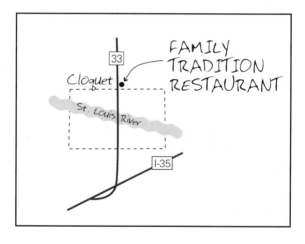

816 Sunnyside Dr. (Hwy 53), Cloquet, MN 55720
Hours: Everyday 6 a.m. - 9 p.m.
         Closed Easter, Thanksgiving, Christmas
Breakfast all day
Children's menu
No smoking
Cash, check or credit cards
Phone: 218-879-1210

C

COTTON

Sue's Sweet Shop

Though the village of Cotton is hardly a slow down on Highway 53, caution is advised to remain alert for the traffic generated by the goings and comings from Sue's Sweet Shop. As Jackie Gleason was fond of saying "how sweet it is."

For 16 years, Sue's has been preparing the perfect pie. No artist can compete with the beauty of these marvelous creations surpassed only by their taste. From French Silk to Sour Cream Raisin or Apple Mincemeat, the variety is startling. Other goodies include cinnamon or pecan rolls, bars, danish, strudel and turnovers. All cooking and baking is homemade.

It's not only the sweets which attract and fill this little cafe. Basic breakfasts, with pancakes of their own reputation, are followed by lunches that feature fresh sandwiches, homemade soups and chili or a fresh salad. Specials such as a pork roast dinner are served every day.

Sue's is a favorite destination for a large community of customers.

For 16 years Sue's has been preparing the perfect pie. No artist can compete with the beauty of these marvelous creations.

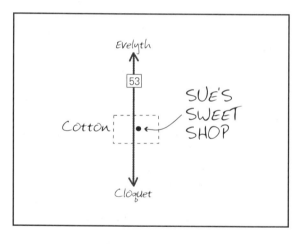

State Hwy 53, Cotton, MN 55724

Hours: Winter: Mon - Sun 7 a.m. - 7 p.m.
　　　　Summer: Mon - Sun 7 a.m. - 8 p.m.
　　　　Closed major Holidays

Breakfast all day

Smoking in designated area

Cash or check only

Phone: 218-482-3281

CROSBY

CUYUNA COUNTRY

Heartland Kitchen

The diner scouting "culinary America" in the Crosby lakes and woods area, should head for the Heartland Kitchen.

Hosts Maureen and Jim Christopher, take special pride in preparing the finest foods. This is not an eatery of adventure but rather of high quality basic dishes. For example, their Sunday brunch, which begins at 9 a.m. features pit roasted ham. This is supplemented with roasted Black Angus at 11 a.m. for the traditional breakfast and lunch buffet.

Breakfast entrees include farm fresh egg omelettes and the general morning selections. A long list of sandwiches and platters follow for lunch, with a complete dinner menu which includes a choice of potatoes, salad or soup and bread stick.

You know that a place as nice as the Heartland Kitchen is not going to let you down on dessert and a full selection of pies, ice-cream, sundaes and special desserts are always in demand.

In terms of atmosphere, a number of local artists have homemade wares on display and for sale. Crafts include carving, pictures, candles and holiday decorations to mention a few.

Their Sunday brunch, which begins at 9 a.m. features pit roasted ham.

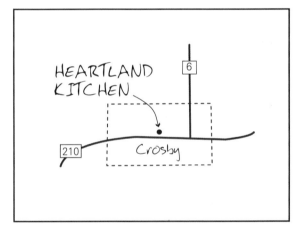

131 W. Main St., Crosby, MN 56441-1428

Hours: Mon - Sat 7 a.m. - 8 p.m.
         Sun 7 a.m. - 7 p.m.
         (extended hours in summer)
         Closed Christmas

Breakfast served all day (no pancakes or French toast after 10 a.m.)

Children's menu

Smoking in designated area

Cash or check only

Phone: 218-546-5746

DULUTH

Duluth Grill

Duluth Grill

The gang at "Cheers" would be at home at the Duluth Grill. You can just about hear the crowd chanting "Norm!" when you walk in the front door of Duluth's most popular eatery.

The breakfast menu is just the start of a great selection. To begin the day, choices include a variety of egg and meat dishes or the traditional buttermilk pancakes and French toast. However it's really the omelettes and specialties where the menu takes off. A build-your-own, everything, hash-brown, or taco selection are on the omelette side, while hash, The Grill's Combo, hash browns, biscuits and gravy and eggs Benedict are among the special selections. All are at prices nice to the wallet.

At lunch the Grill's selections represent everything expected at a classic diner. Naturally, burger choices are number one on the list. Beyond the catchy names there exists real substance to the Ariel, Skyline Inferno, Northern, Railmelt and Duluth Grill Dairy Burger selections. In addition the Grill features Chargrilled Chicken Sandwiches and a variety of Specialties.

For dinner the menu adds a nice collection of steaks, poultry, fish, international entrees, and a comprehensive choice of salads. Dinners include choice of potato, rice pilaf, soup or salad, vegetable and roll.

The gang at "Cheers" would be at home at the Duluth Grill. You can just about hear the crowd chanting "Norm!"

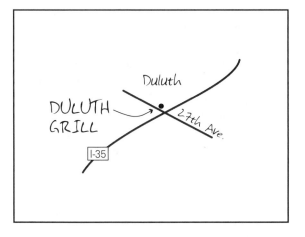

118 S. 27th Ave. West, Duluth, MN 55806
Hours: Open everyday
        Sun - Thurs 6 a.m. - 8 p.m.
        Fri - Sat 6 a.m. - 10 p.m.
Breakfast served all day
Children's menu
Smoking in designated area
Credit cards accepted
Phone: 218-727-1527

DULUTH (PIKE LAKE)

Gallaghers Country Cafe

Now owned by Jim and Linda Gallagher, Duluth's home-style cafe is the product of Jim's parents' efforts who started the restaurant in 1947.

This is a family oriented, home cooking type of place where foods are served in a dining area given to the comfort of soft gray accented by burgundy and green booths. Every Tuesday night is family night when kids ten and under eat for $1.00 and entertainment is provided.

Breakfast offerings include the usual variety of pancakes, egg dishes, meats and potatoes. Their homemade muffins are a specialty.

The lunch and dinner menus are large. Plate lunches (reasonably priced), 16 sandwiches (not including the burger choices or melts) make for some serious decision time. When dinner time rolls around, Gallaghers offers a fine selection of meats, chicken and a long list of fish entrees. Their choice of fresh salads is a perfect selection for the lite appetite.

Tuesday night is family night when kids ten and under eat for $1.00.

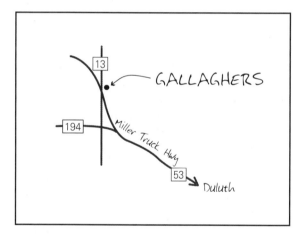

5671 Miller Trunk Hwy., Duluth, MN 55811
Hours: Mon - Thurs 11a.m. - 9 p.m.
          Fri - Sat 6 a.m. - 9 p.m.
          Sun 7 a.m. - 8 p.m.
          Closed Christmas Day
Breakfast served to 11:30 a.m. Fri - Sun
Children's menu
Smoking in designated area
No credit cards
Phone: 218-729-7100

DULUTH

LAKE AVENUE CAFE

Lake Avenue Cafe

The husband and wife team, of Patrick Cross and Mary Ann Immerfall, has established a wonderful little restaurant located in the Historic DeWitt-Seitz Marketplace.

The building itself of 1909 vintage, is a former manufacturing site (at one time a mattress factory) and now home to a collection of boutique shops which are perfect for a before or after dining stroll.

The cafe's menu offers some wonderful and original creations. Every month or so they change their specialties which allows them to use seasonal ingredients. Thai Chili, a composition of over 20 ingredients, is a local contest winner and deserves serious thought as an entrée of choice when offered. Other temptations include Saffron Linguine with spicy seafood, pork chop with mustard and sour cream or pasta plates with a choice of both pastas and sauces (a create-your-own type of meal).

Sandwiches, a soup du jour and specialty pizzas like pesto or margarita are popular lunch choices.

*Thai Chili, a composition of
over twenty ingredients, is a local
contest winner.*

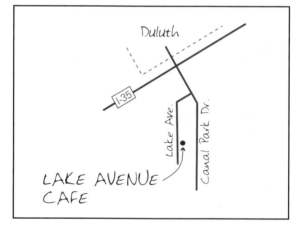

394 Lake Ave. So., Duluth, MN 55802
Hours: Sun - Thurs 11 a.m. - 9 p.m.
　　　　Fri - Sat 11 a.m. - 10 p.m.
　　　　Closed major Holidays
No smoking
Credit cards accepted
Phone: 218-722-2355

DULUTH (NORTH SHORE)

Lakeview Castle

Lakeview Castle

Lakeview Castle is a unique dining experience. Situated on the North Shore Drive, 20 minutes from Duluth, the exterior design features a moat like an entrance between two turrets, with a beautiful bank of windows overlooking Lake Superior.

The restaurant's ambiance is best interpreted as formal-casual, done in muted tones with a large stone wall fireplace as a focal point.

Lakeview Castle itself was established in 1914 and the restaurant has a business history dating back 38 years.

Serving the finest in steaks and seafood, house specialties include Greek entrees. Highlights include a pepper steak, Greek Dolmathes and Spanakopta. The menu selection is varied from fresh fish to homemade pizza.

Lunches emphasize large burgers, homemade soups, breads and elegant desserts.

Notable breakfast entrees are their homemade pancakes and omelettes. Also recommended are homemade rye and cinnamon toasts.

*Highlights include a pepper steak,
Greek Dolmathes and Spanakopta.*

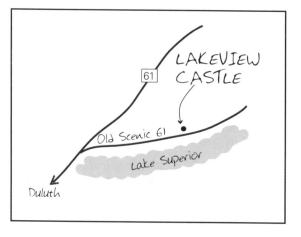

5135 No. Scenic Shore Dr., Duluth, MN 55804
Hours: Summer: Daily 8 a.m. - 10 p.m.
        Winter: Mon - Fri - call for hrs
                Sat - Sun 8 a.m. - 10 p.m.
        Open daily except Christmas
Breakfast served to 12 noon
Children's menu
Smoking in designated area
Credit cards accepted
Phone: 218-525-1014, 218-525-1963

ELY

Britton's Cafe

Britton's Cafe

For anyone in Ely in need of police assistance it might not hurt to look in Britton's Cafe. This is where the guardians of the peace, as well as local citizenry, find home cooking at its finest. It's been that way for over 25 years.

Begin the day with their (soon to be) famous stuffed hash browns. This wonderful dish adds to the basic potato a mixture of ham with American and mozzarella cheese. Breakfast choices are made difficult by the array of homemade bakery items. Selections include long johns, caramel and frosted rolls, raised donuts and bismarcks.

Lunches include burgers, hot sandwiches (beef, pork or turkey), croissants and salads, and a long list of chicken alternatives.

Dinner choices are rotated daily among a page-long list of favorites. Examples include meat loaf, ham au gratin and Mexican specialties. Sundays feature roast turkey or ham.

This is where the guardians of the peace, as well as local citizenry, find home cooking at its finest.

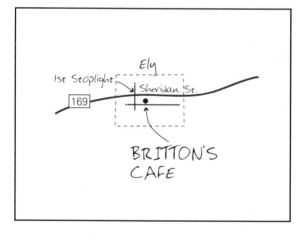

5 E. Chapman St., Ely, MN 55731
Hours: Winter: Mon - Fri 6 a.m. - 7 p.m.
          Sat - Sun 6 a.m. - 2 p.m.
      Summer: Mon - Sat 5 a.m. - 7 p.m.
          Sun 6 a.m. - 2 p.m.
Breakfast served until 11:30 a.m.
Children's menu
Smoking in designated area
No credit cards
Phone: 218-365-3195

ELY

Minglewood Cafe

In Minnesota's area of northern lights the Minglewood Cafe prepares a diverse selection of fresh homemade foods.

Transforming an older home into an existing cafe, owner Laurie Larson prepares entrees to accommodate every appetite from vegetarian to those on special diets.

Breakfast choices include eggs, garlic sausage patties, a Spanish omelette with Chorizo sausage and three "hash" selections. There is a nice reasonably priced "Early Bird" breakfast buffet from 6 a.m. Monday through Friday. Luncheon dishes are comprised of hot and cold sandwiches, homemade soups and salads or a Mexican selection, accompanied by their own made-from-scratch salsa. Most seasonings are from their garden fresh herbs.

Ely is a town dedicated to tourists. As a gateway to Boundary Waters Canoe Area Wilderness, the local outfitters provide camping gear, food, canoes and fishing tips. Village attractions include the International Wolf Center, museums and one-of-a-kind shops.

Laurie Larson prepares entrees to accommodate every appetite from vegetarian to those on special diets.

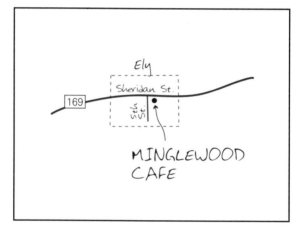

528 E. Sheridan St., Ely, MN 55731
Hours: Mon - Sun 6 a.m. - 3 p.m.
            Mid April to October
Breakfast served to 11 a.m. (all day on Sun)
Children's menu
Smoking: outside patio only
Credit cards accepted
Phone: 218-365-3398

EMBARRASS

Four Corners
C ◆ A ◆ F ◆ E

Four Corners Cafe

There is generally a reason when a parking lot is full. Though there is some gas pumped at the Four Corners location, the carriage occupants are usually busy eating and socializing in the cafe as opposed to attending motoring needs.

This down-home, friendly, knotty-pine little establishment has been serving up the fundamentals in a truck stop sort of way for the last 25 years.

Steak and eggs with hash browns and toast, and the Everything omlette, will satisfy most everyone; and of course the usual choices of eggs, pancakes and French toast are on the menu.

For lunch there is the Jumbo Burger, Super Burger, or just the burger and a Patty Melt. Other appeals include a pizza burger and Grilled Steak Hoagie.

Dinner choices include shrimp, fish, walleye (this is Minnesota), chicken, with a Thursday and Saturday night prime rib special from 4 - 7 p.m.

This down-home, friendly, knotty-pine establishment has been serving up the fundamentals for 25 years.

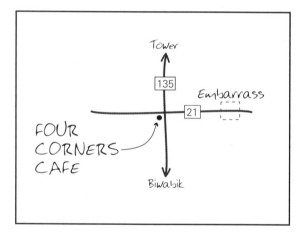

7491 Hwy 135 N., Embarrass, MN 55732

Hours: Mon - Fri 6 a.m. - 7 p.m.
        Sat 7 a.m. - 7 p.m., Sun 8 a.m. - 7 p.m.

Breakfast all day (no pancakes or French toast
        after 11:30 a.m.)

Smoking in designated area

Credit cards accepted

Phone: 218-984-2055

EVELYTH

Deluxe Cafe

In a way, appearances are be deceiving. The Deluxe is centrally located on Evelyth's main street (Grant Avenue) and appears to be a smallish restaurant, hidden in the middle of the block. Reality is, however, that the restaurant is multi-roomed, cleverly and pleasingly decorated to produce a charm and character which belies the rather humble exterior.

Under the 26 year guidance of owner Harold Ebnet, the restaurant has grown in both scope and reputation. Service to the community is provided by participation in the "meal on wheels" program, and the hosting of numerous events even including ski teams who arrive from nearby Giants Ridge.

Foods are homemade including all baked goods. The breakfast menu features traditional egg and meat dishes served with fresh American fried potatoes. Pancakes, omelettes and French toast are popular selections which can be ordered with sides of bacon, ham or sausage.

Lunches center on homemade soups and sandwiches. There is a winning choice of burgers, melts and croissants. Deluxe favorites include gyros, a steak or chicken philly, grilled Reuben or a toasted beef and onion.

A variety of dinner options are available. Veal Parmigiana, Blackened Chicken Alfredo, liver and onions or steaks are among the choices. Soups and entrée salads are also on the menu.

Cleverly and pleasingly decorated to produce a charm and character which belies the rather humble exterior.

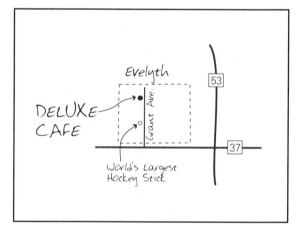

225 Grant Ave., Evelyth, MN 55734

Hours: Mon - Fri 7 a.m. - 8 p.m.
          Sat 8 a.m. - 8 p.m., Sun 8 a.m. - 3 p.m.
          Open every day – call for Holiday hours

Breakfast served all day

Children's menu

Smoking in designated area

Credit cards accepted

Phone: 218-744-4960

FINLAND

Trestle Inn

The Trestle Inn, located on the Tomahawk Trail, is a diversion into the forests of northern Minnesota with a purpose. Here the explorer experiences the atmosphere which can only be created by a restaurant constructed of 300-year-old timbers from an abandoned railroad trestle and some really good food.

These are lumberjack type "eatin's." Substantial food of quality and quantity. Weekend breakfasts (winter only) are identified by their special Trestle Tators followed by flapjacks, French toast and the regular egg and meat choices.

Lunches include an assortment of mainstay sandwiches highlighted by the Trestle Burger – claimed to be the best you've ever had. Dinner entrees take in steaks, shrimp, walleye and all-you-can-eat BBQ pork ribs on Saturday and Sunday. There is also a Friday fish fry during the summer months.

Area activities are seasonal from snowmobiling, hiking, fishing and biking to horseback riding.

These are lumberjack type "eatin's."

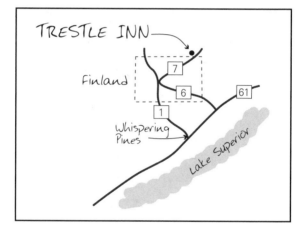

Lake Co. Rte. 7 (P.O. Box 548), Finland, MN 55603

Hours: Winter: Mon - Thurs 12 noon - 8 p.m.
               Fri 12 noon - 10 p.m.
               Sat 9 a.m. - 11 p.m.
               Sun 9 a.m. - 8 p.m.
        Summer: Sun - Thurs 12 noon - 9 p.m.
                Fri - Sat 12 noon - 10 p.m.
        Closed April
        Open weekends 3rd Sun Oct. - Dec. 26

Breakfast served to 11 a.m. Sat and Sun

Smoking in designated area

Cash only

Phone: not available

GARRISON

Vicki's Seguchie Inn

Just to the south of Garrison, Highway 169 signage for the Seguchie Inn announces "We serve really hungry people!" There is truth in advertising.

A genuinely old restaurant, there is a spirit of fish tales well told. The interior is wooden and worn with a feeling of comfort.

Portions are big from breakfast to burgers. The menu is compact to include the basics. Day openers include eggs with seasoned potatoes or 'cakes and meat. A popular luncheon choice is the Seguchie burger, a full 1/2 pounder with two cheeses and two sauces served on a grilled sourdough roll. Hot sandwiches, spaghetti and walleye are also tempting choices, with pizza and broasted chicken filling out the menu.

Popular luncheon choice: the Seguchie burger, a $1/2$ pounder with two cheeses, two sauces on a grilled sourdough roll.

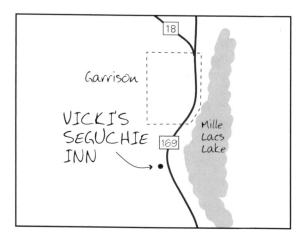

Rte 169 (HCRI, Box 88), Garrison, MN 56450
Hours: Sun - Thurs 7 a.m. - 8 p.m.
       Fri - Sat 7 a.m. - 10 p.m.
Breakfast served until 10:30 a.m.
Children's and seniors' menu
Smoking in designated area
Credit cards accepted
Phone: 320-692-4140

G

GARRISON

Svododa's Spotlite Restaurant & Bakery

Garrison, on the western shore of Lake Mille Lacs, is at the center of the area's attractions. Easily accessible are activities ranging from golf to gaming and, of course, fishing.

Mille Lacs, at 132,516 acres, is one of the state's premier destinations for anglers looking for Minnesota's favorite fish, the walleye.

Since 1948 the cafe, now known as Svoboda's has been satisfying the appetites of this busy, busy area. With the adjacent bakery and ice-cream shop, the restaurant has a full range of foods ready for the customer. The atmosphere is north-woods knotty pine.

"Good Mornings" start with a fine selection of eggs, pancakes and such, omelettes and sweets. A full luncheon menu includes an agreeable balance between sandwiches and burgers with all bakery items on premise. Cafe specialties include a steak sandwich, ham sandwich delux and a dieter's delight breast of chicken.

Dinners, which are complemented with either soup or salad, potatoes and roll, include walleye, chicken, steaks and country fried steaks with gravy.

With the adjacent bakery and ice-cream shop, the restaurant has a full range of foods ready for the customer.

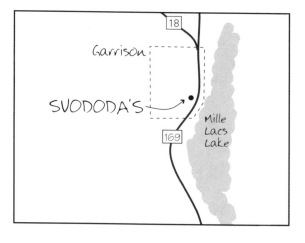

111 Madison St., Garrison, MN 56450

Hours: Mon - Thurs 5:30 a.m. - 3 p.m.
   Fri - Sun 5:30 a.m. - 9 p.m.
   May close Holidays and mid Nov. - mid Dec.
   Call for details

Breakfast served anytime

Children's and 60+ menu

Smoking in designated area

Credit cards accepted

Phone: 320-692-4567

G

GILBERT

Memory Lane Cafe

Proprietor Marlene Foster chose to name her home-style little cafe Memory Lane to reflect the décor she adopted for the restaurant's character. The use of antiques such as coffee pots, cow bells, and even a wooden ox yoke create a homespun sense of dining.

The menu sticks to the basics. Egg and meat combos, hash browns, 'cakes, English muffins, caramel rolls and a create-your-own omelette are the breakfast essentials. For lunch the choices include burgers, sandwiches, baskets and hot sandwiches. Roast beef, turkey, soups and gravies are all homemade.

Our Memory Lane expands the dinner side. A full list of traditional choices including ribs, liver and onions and ham steak are supplemented by specials, a bit of Italy and a Touch of Ol' Mexico. The diner has a choice of spaghetti, tostados, chimichangas, Italian sausage, Polish sausage or a ham & burger sandwich.

For dessert Marlene offers fried ice cream, sundaes and homemade pies or cakes.

Proprietor Marlene Foster chose to name her home-style little cafe Memory Lane to reflect the décor she adopted for the restaurants character.

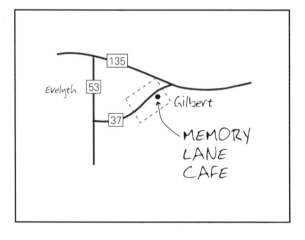

223 Broadway No. (Hwy 37), Gilbert, MN 55741
Hours: Sun - Thurs 7 a.m. - 9 p.m.
        Fri 7 a.m. - 11 p.m.
        Closed only on Christmas Day
Breakfast served all day
Children's menu
Smoking in designated area
Cash or check only
Phone: 218-749-8402

GRAND MARAIS

Sven & Ole's.

Sven & Ole's

A landmark, Sven & Ole's has nourished the North Shore devotee since 1981.

With a reputation for artistic expression, the harbor village of Grand Marais is home to shops and galleries while forming a gateway to the resorts and activities of the likable Gunflint Trail.

For pizza lovers, Sven & Ole's is a must do. Their made-from-fresh-ingredients pie can be ordered with either a thick or thin crust. Supplemental additions include deli sandwiches, burgers and hoagies with pasta, homemade soups and fresh-to-order salads, also on the menu.

The environment is a business-like, busy, and customer-friendly pizza pie eatery.

For pizza lovers, Sven & Ole's is a must do.

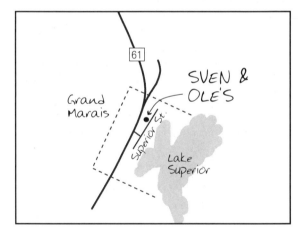

9 W. Wisconsin St., Grand Marais, MN 55604

Hours: Daily 11 a.m. - 9 p.m.
Summer: 9 a.m. - 10 p.m.
Closed Easter, Thanksgiving, Christmas

No smoking

Credit cards: V, MC, D

Phone: 218-387-1713

GRAND MARAIS

Trail Center Lodge

Where will you find that Rhubarb Malt? To discover this unusual treat you will need to be on the Gunflint Trail. Some 29 miles "in" from Grand Marais, the Trail Center Lodge dishes out their special variation on some basic foods, including malts.

Breakfast on Santa Fe grits, walleye or bratwurst and eggs. Really need a Goober Burger for lunch? The Lodge is the place. However, if peanut butter and mayo on your burger is not exactly your first choice, there are a dozen other burger combinations. They also have a Killer Chili, Meatless Taco Salad (or a Taco Salad), plus lunch specials.

Among the dinner choices are Iowa pork chops, Italian fried chicken and either a pork rib or shrimp combo.

Fit into a refurbished 1930s sawmill, the Lodge's innovative menu and plentiful portions will satisfy the hungry appetite.

*A refurbished 1930's sawmill, the
Lodge's innovative menu and portions
will satisfy the hungry appetite.*

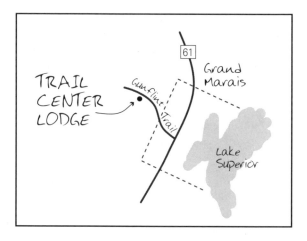

7611 Gunflint Trail, Grand Marais, MN 55604

Hours: Mon - Thurs 8 a.m. - 9 p.m.
        Fri - Sat 8 a.m. - 10 p.m.
        Sun 8 a.m. - 9 p.m.
        Open Holidays

Breakfast served until 11 a.m. weekdays, noon on
        weekends

Children's menu

Smoking in designated area

Credit cards accepted

Phone: 218-388-2214

GRAND RAPIDS

HOME TOWN CAFE

Home Town Cafe

Grand Rapids, the birth place of Judy Garland, honors her with a museum and annual festival. The area is also the destination of those who enjoy the numerous resorts on the area's 1,000 lakes and the programs available in conjunction with the Chippewa National Forest.

Located in downtown Grand Rapids, the new owner of the Home Town Cafe, Marsha Niehoff takes pride in her homemade (from scratch) foods including pies, real mashed potatoes and even maidrite (perhaps also known as "loose burger") sandwiches. Their motto is "real food at real prices." Particular emphasis is given to fast service since the regulars don't have lunch "hours" and appreciate the attentiveness.

The atmosphere is comfortable with a folksy decor and most customers are on a first name basis. Ample parking is available behind the restaurant with an entrance at the rear facing the public parking area.

Homemade (from scratch) foods including pies, real mashed potatoes and even maidrite sandwiches.

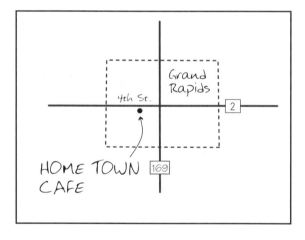

18 N.W. 4th St., Grand Rapids, MN 55744

Hours: Mon - Sat 5 a.m. - 3 p.m.
Closed Sundays and Holidays

Breakfast served 5 a.m. - 11 a.m. Mon - Fri,
all day Sat

Children's menu

Smoking in designated area

No credit cards

Phone: 218-326-8646

GRANDY

Brass Rail

Chicken, chicken, chicken. Oh sure this legendary little cafe prepares some other very tempting dishes (well worth a try from time to time) but it's the Broasted Chicken that has the crowds returning as they have for the last 30 years.

With a wide selection of combinations on their chicken-to-go list, it is rumored that owners Ennis and Donna Biggins once brought an order of chicken out to a waiting car stuck in traffic.

The family orientated cafe is housed in a 100-year old building with the tin ceiling and oil brass bar rail still in tact.

The most popular item includes the broasted chicken, broasted potato, cole slaw and toast combination. Don't order anything more than the quarter-chicken unless you're extremely hungry.

The menu also lists haddock and shrimp plus a full list of sandwiches including chicken (of course), ham, fish, a BLT and burgers. Side orders and pizza are also available.

It's the Broasted Chicken that has the crowds returning as they have for the last 30 years.

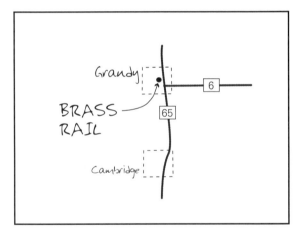

36868 Hwy 65 N.E., Grandy, MN 55029

Hours: Mon - Fri 11 a.m. - 10 p.m.
          Sat 11 a.m. - 12 midnight
          Sun 12 noon - 10 p.m.
          Closed Christmas Day, New Year's Day

Smoking in designated area

Cash or check only

Phone: 763-689-9965

H

HARRIS

Valkommen till Var

Kaffe Stuga

Kaffe Stuga

While it may be easy to entirely miss the little town of Harris (pop. 843), it's difficult to miss the line outside the Kaffe Stuga - especially on Sundays from opening at 10:45 a.m. to closing at 2 p.m.

As their reputation for the quality of the home-style food grows, there is a steady traffic flow from the "cities" to this little ol' cafe.

The reason? Take, for example, the Sunday menu Roast beef, roast pork, baked breaded pork chops and dressing, fried chicken, baked ham, BBQ ribs, walleye, roast turkey and dressing, plus note mashed potatoes and gravy. So expect a wait to be seated!

The proud ownership in the Ramberg family goes back some 25 years with the restaurant's Swedish decor supplied by Janet and Darell's daughter and son-in-law, who display their Scandinavian products and clocks in the restaurant.

There is a full breakfast selection, and lunch features the "Stuga Burger." Homemade pies and other desserts such as bread pudding and carrot cake are made daily.

On a seasonal note, mark your calendar for the second Tuesday of December when the cafe offers their Lutefisk Buffet which features lutefisk (naturally), homemade potato sausage, baked ham and Swedish meatballs with all the trimmings.

As their reputation for the quality of the home-style food grows, there is a steady traffic flow from the "cities" to this little ol' cafe.

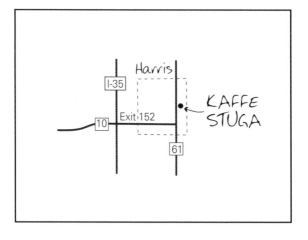

43831 Forest Blvd., Harris, MN 55032

Hours: Mon - Fri 7:30 a.m. - 7:30 p.m.
        Sat 8 a.m. - 7:30 p.m.
        Sun 10:45 a.m. - 2 p.m.
        Closed Holidays

Breakfast served to 11 a.m.

Smoking in designated area

Cash only

Phone: 651-674-9958

H

HOYT LAKES

Vaughn's Restaurant

The town of Hoyt Lakes (pop. 2,348) is located on Colby lake in the Arrowhead region. With access to I-35 at Aurora, MN, the area is a sports activities center. The city boasts of excellent fishing, hiking and camping in the summer and hosts an annual snowmobile rally in the winter.

Vaghn's Restaurant carries the northwoods theme using "woodsy" tones and decor. The small town cafe is busy with tourists and locals, providing a family style dining atmosphere with ample quantities of fine foods.

Breakfast fare is traditional with omelettes, waffles and French toast. Lunch is basically soups and pies. Dinner specials includes Wednesday night pizza buffet and an excellent walleye Friday fish fry.

*Dinner special includes Wednesday
night pizza buffet, and an excellent
walleye Friday fish fry.*

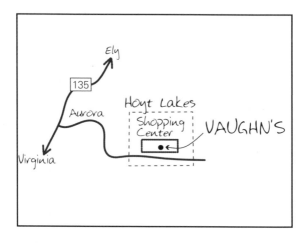

255 Kennedy Memorial Dr., Hoyt Lakes, MN 55750

Hours: Mon - Thurs 6 a.m. - 8 p.m.
        Fri - Sat 6 a.m. - 10 p.m.
        Sun 6 a.m. - 8 p.m.
        Call for Holiday schedule

Breakfast served to 11 a.m. weekdays,
        1 p.m. weekends

Children's menu

No credit cards

Phone: 218-225-3331

INTERNATIONAL FALLS

Sandy's Place

Sandy's Place

Crossing the border, visiting or just plain hungry, the spot to be is Sandy's Place. The "Falls" itself is a popular access for the Voyageur National Park area named after the French Canadian fur traders who initially explored the region in the late 1700s. One of the more popular annual events is their January Icebox Days which provides a number of family events.

Since this is a land made for big appetites, Sandy's serves up abundant platefuls of homemade foods. Platter-sized, homemade pancakes are a great way to start the day or the biscuits and gravy will also numb the hunger pangs. Omelettes and egg and meat selections fill out the breakfast choices.

A nice choice of sandwiches, burgers and hot sandwiches with homemade mashed potatoes are available for lunch. Real French fries can be added to a burger or sandwich choice. Lunch specials, changing from baked ham on Mondays to meatballs on Friday come in three sizes - small, medium or large. The Turkey Tuesday (with all the trimmings) is a popular favorite.

Homemade pies are a specialty. Sandy uses her mother's recipes to create these wonderful desserts.

The atmosphere is homey with the woody interior providing a warm feeling to the spotlessly clean cafe.

Since this is a land made for big appetites, Sandy's serves up abundant platefuls of homemade foods.

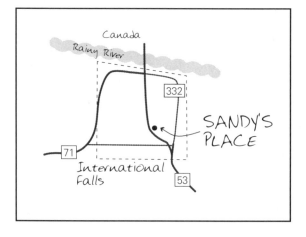

1510-3rd Ave., International Falls, MN 56649

Hours: Mon - Fri 5:30 a.m. - 4 p.m.
         Sat 5:30 a.m. - 2 p.m.
         Closed Sundays and Holidays

Breakfast served all day

Children's menu

Smoking in designated area

No credit cards

Phone: 218-285-9108

LITTLE FALLS

The Black & White Hamburger Shop

The original 1931 Black and White diner has been transformed by present owner, Ron Lyschik, into what might be best summarized as a cultural icon.

Using fixtures, counter space and cabinetry from the original diner with works of local artists representing various disciplines, and signage from bygone community businesses, the little cafe is now a town meeting place. Ron has also added a book department functioning as a depository for used books, displayed in the cafe's numerous bookcases. The sale prices of .25 to .50 simply cover the recycling costs.

The Black and White Cafe has also evolved into a full service restaurant. Breakfasts are highlighted by their homemade pancakes and generously proportioned omelettes. Their breakfast special includes a full choice of meat, eggs, potatoes, toast and beverage. Lunch is a major component of the Black and White creative menu featuring specialty sandwiches and salads.

Though adventuresome in part, the menu still provides the basics. The best in meat for burgers, fresh French fries and malts are popular choices.

The area itself has some wonderful attractions, including the boyhood home of Charles Lindbergh and other late 1800s landmarks and buildings of distinction.

Using fixtures from the original diner, works of local artists and signage from bygone community businesses, the little cafe is now a town meeting place.

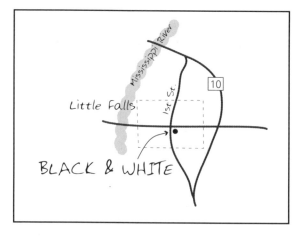

116 S.E. 1st St., Little Falls, MN 56345
Hours: Mon - Fri 7 a.m. - 7 p.m.
        Sat 7 a.m. - 2 p.m., Sun 8 a.m. - 1 p.m.
        Closed major holidays
Breakfast served all day
Children's menu
No smoking
Cash and all major credit cards
Phone: 320-632-5374

L

LITTLEFORK

MOTEL and RV PARK

Home Town Cafe

Appropriately named, the Home Town Cafe may best be described by its nostalgic appeal. This is the manner and character of surroundings experienced in times past. Lace curtains, mix and match furniture and Littlefork's memorabilia provide the essential environment.

The marvelous homey beanery results from the efforts of owners Laura Ingram (mother), Marsha Winner (daughter) and Richard Winner (son-in law). Their careful attention promises a meal that is both comfortable and satisfying.

Their menu is a little surprising, anchored by a nice assortment of fresh baked pies, breads, muffins and rolls. The breakfast entrees highlight Cloverdale ham, bacon and sausage to accompany the egg and 'cake choices. A palatable selection of sandwiches, salads and burgers of beef, pork, chicken and fish.

Friday and Saturday evening meals are complemented by a soup and salad bar, with a prime rib special on Friday. As a tasting option their Little Mexico Specials are available everyday.

Their menu is a little surprising, anchored by an assortment of fresh baked pies, breads, muffins and rolls.

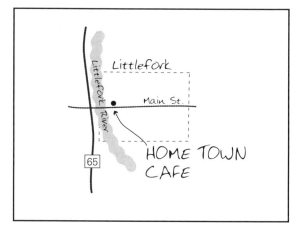

112 Main St., Littlefork, MN 56653
      (by the bridge over Littlefork River)
Hours: Mon - Sat 9 a.m. - 2 p.m.
       Closed Sunday
       Call for reservations as hours may vary
Smoking in designated area
Cash or check only
Phone: 218-278-4788

LUTSEN

Cascade Lodge Restaurant

The restaurant is part of the Cascade Lodge Resort overlooking Lake Superior and surrounded by the Cascade River State Park. The lodge and Restaurant began its service in 1926.

With a large stone fireplace, exposed wooden beams and spectacular views of Lake Superior, the atmosphere of the restaurant is warm and comfortable. The environs also include wagon wheel lights with trophy fish and animal exhibits.

Access to the park assures the visitor year round activities such as hiking, cross country skiing, mountain biking and snowmobiling.

Their menu offers a fine variety of breakfast, lunch and dinner options. Omelettes and pancakes begin the day, followed by burgers and sandwiches for lunch, with steak, seafood and pasta choices for dinner. Wild rice soup is a popular and well noted favorite.

Wild rice soup is a popular and well noted favorite.

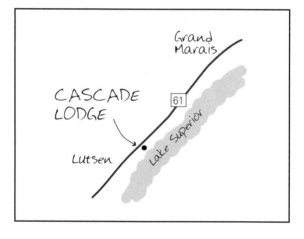

3719 W. Hwy 61, Lutsen, MN 55612
Hours: Spring/Fall: (5/15 - 6/30 and 9/8 - 10/17):
        Sun - Thurs 7:30 a.m. - 8 p.m.
        Fri - Sat 7:30 a.m. - 9 p.m.
    Summer: (7/1 - Labor Day)
        Sun - Thurs 7 a.m. - 9 p.m.
        Fri - Sat 7 a.m. - 10 p.m.
    Winter: Mon - Sun 7:30 a.m. - 8 p.m.
Breakfast served until 2 p.m.
Children's menu
Credit cards: V, MC, D
Phone: 218-387-1112, 800-322-9543

MOOSE LAKE

Wyndtree Restaurant

At this spic and span restaurant, the traveler is treated to the best in homemade goodies. Helen, at age 78, brings together all her baking skills to create pies, caramel and cinnamon rolls, as well as special bran muffins. The buttermilk pancakes come from a local heritage cookbook recipe.

Eggs and Things are featured on the breakfast menu along with biscuits and gravy and the Wyndtree "works" omelette.

The large lunch selection includes subs, melts and lite sandwiches. Among the dinner specials accompanied by real mashed potatoes are meat loaf (recipe not for sale), liver and onions and hot sandwiches. Salad toppings of choice are their homemade ranch or cheese dressings.

The buttermilk pancakes come from a local heritage cookbook recipe.

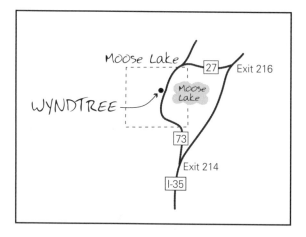

300 S. Arrowhead Lane, Moose Lake, MN 55767

Hours: 6 a.m. - 9 p.m. daily
        Winter: Mon - Thurs 6 a.m. - 8 p.m.
        Call for Holiday hours

Breakfast served all day

Children's menu

No Smoking

Credit cards: V, MC, D

Phone: 218-485-8712

MORA

Grandma's Kitchen

Grandma's Kitchen

Grandma's Kitchen is the city's purveyor of home-made meals. For the last five years, owner Randy and Jan Sward have been preparing "real" foods including their own BBQ sauce, salad dressings, pies and rolls.

In "putting out good food at a reasonable price," the cafe's success is evident from the crowded parking lot. This is a busy cafe. Crowds begin with their breakfast specials, followed by lunch with choices of sandwiches, salads and burgers. Dinner specials include meat loaf, chicken, liver and onions or spaghetti. Homemade mashed potatoes are a specialty.

Locally the Kanabec History Center is a visitor focal point. The city's Swedish roots are evident in the museum which features immigrant heritage and culture.

The cafe draws it atmosphere from its business and wildlife paintings. There are some locally made crafts and handmade rugs for sale.

In "putting out good food at a reasonable price," the cafe's success is evident from the crowded parking lot.

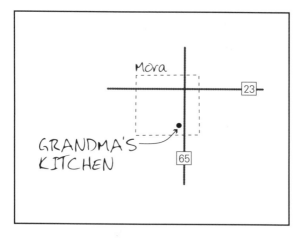

825 S. Hwy 65, Mora, MN 55051
Hours: Mon-Fri 5:30 a.m. - 8:30 p.m.
   Sat 8:30 a.m. - 9 p.m.
   Sun 6 a.m. - 9 p.m.
   Closed some Holidays
Breakfast served to 11:30 a.m.
Smoking in designated area
No credit cards
Phone: 320-679-5794

ORR

Orr Cafe

The Orr Cafe has a tradition spanning some 50 years. Rebuilt in 1996 on a large bay of Pelican Lake, owners Bob and Loretta Anola have been created a sparkling new restaurant. The cafe was designed with a view to the outside using large windows with bright colors of green and white to accent the country charm.

Orr, with its proximity to the Canadian border, provides access to Minnesota's only National Park, Voyageurs, and the Boundary Waters Canoe Area Wilderness. Seasonal activities include summertime fishing, boating and canoeing with winter adventures to include dog-sledding, ice fishing and snowmobiling.

Energy to attack the outdoors begins with their lumberjack special of either steak or pork chops with eggs and potatoes. Biscuits and gravy are a Saturday highlight and homemade twists, donuts and cinnamon rolls are made fresh daily.

Baskets (shrimp, burger or chicken) are nice luncheon options, with diverse dinner choices which include walleye or a ham steak. The dinner menu adds specials such as meat loaf, roast turkey and spaghetti. Their chicken dumpling soup, an every Thursday addition, has acquired a large following.

Their chicken dumpling soup,
an every Thursday addition,
has acquired a large following.

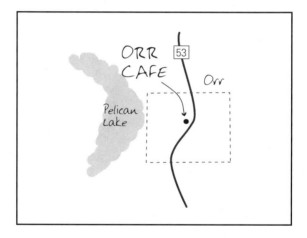

4549 Hwy 53, Orr, MN 55771

Hours: Winter: Mon - Sat 5 a.m. - 8 p.m.
                      Sun 6 a.m. - 8 p.m.
             Summer: Mon - Sat 5 a.m. - 9 p.m.
                      Sun 6 a.m. - 8 p.m.
             Holidays - call for hours

Breakfast served until 11 a.m.

Smoking in designated area

Cash only

Phone: not available

PALISADE

Palisade Cafe

Pure America in Minnesota's northwoods. The Palisade Cafe is a genuine informal family cafe with warmth, charm and unbelievably low prices. Though the old building has recently been updated, the original hand crafted wood counter with its eight stools and original porcelain feet remain. The walls and ceiling cove are painted tin.

The friendly staff and boisterous atmosphere cannot be adequately described – it must be enjoyed. This is a family enterprise. Todd as the main cook while older brother Roger is manager, assistant cook, buyer and bookkeeper. Father Wayne buses tables and even does the dishes, (sounds like him, and it is) while Mom bakes, peels potatoes, makes salads and soups, and helps wait on tables.

The food is vintage home cooking. Breakfast specials include their homemade stuffed hash browns and the "everything" omelettes. Lunches feature old fashioned hamburgers and broasted chicken. The dinner menu varies with people-pleasing choices such as cabbage rolls, lasagna, pork, stuffed peppers or liver and onions. Friday night's fish fry and Thursday's spaghetti are both all-you-can-eat for an unbeatable price. Seniors' specials are even less expensive for a complete dinner including dessert! It is not unusual to find folks from 70 miles around stopping in to enjoy both the food and atmosphere.

Homemade desserts feature bread pudding, pies, cakes, cookies, doughnuts and caramel rolls.

Friday night's fish fry and Thursday's spaghetti are both all-you-can-eat for an unbeatable price.

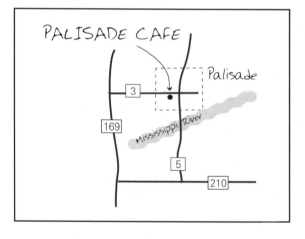

Main St., Palisade, MN 56469

Hours: Summer (5/1 -10/31)
                    Mon - Sat 7 a.m. - 8 p.m.
              Winter 11/1 - 4/30
                    Mon - Thurs 7 a.m. - 7 p.m.
                    Fri - Sat 7 a.m. - 7 p.m.
                    Sun 8 a.m. - 7 p.m.
              Closed Thanksgiving and Christmas Day

Breakfast all day

No smoking areas upon request

Cash only

Phone: 218-845-2214

PINE CITY

Red Shed

On the I-35 corridor south of Hinckley, the Red Shed is an ideal pit stop.

Now in its third generation of family ownership and with members of the fourth working in the cafe, the restaurant has been offering fine food and service for over 30 years.

Daybreak starters include jumbo cinnamon rolls, biscuits and gravy, corned beef, hash and 'cake combos. Breakfast specials normally include variations of their marvelously light Belgian waffles.

Homemade soups and chili anchor the lunch and dinner entrees with the broasted chicken as a popular favorite. Dessert specials include the Shed's well-known bread pudding. Real homemade malts are also available.

The atmosphere resembles an "indoor shed" with seasonal decorations on the major holidays. The exceptional service is provided by a loyal staff color fully attired in red polo shirts with the Shed logo.

Breakfast specials normally include variations of their marvelously light Belgian waffles.

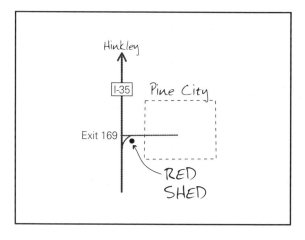

1400 Hillside Ave. (S.E. corner of I-35, Exit 169)
 Pine City, MN 55063
Hours: Winter: Mon - Thurs 7 a.m. - 8 p.m.
         Fri - Sun 7 a.m. - 9 p.m.
        Summer: Mon - Thurs 7 a.m. - 9 p.m.
         Fri - Sun 7 a.m. - 10 p.m.
        Closed Christmas
        Call for Holiday hours
Juniors' and seniors' menu
Smoking in designated area
Credit cards: V, MC, D
Phone: 320-629-3416

PRINCETON

SINCE 1961
K-BOB Cafe
"WHERE FRIENDS MEET TO EAT"

K-Bob Cafe

Since 1961 the Tou family has been operating this vintage cafe in downtown Princeton. Now in their third generation of creating honorable home-style meals, the family remains committed to the finest in simple good foods.

This busy restaurant has gained a wonderful reputation which makes it a frequent stop for out-of-town guests enroute to and from lake homes in the north.

The menu offers a wide variety of home-cooked meals and daily dinner, lunch and breakfast specials. There is a fine selection of salads available as well as homemade soups and chili (in season). Their popular breakfast selections include early-riser and late-riser specials. The Early Bird Breakfasts are available from 5 - 8 a.m. at distinctive prices, and the late-riser menu includes a South of the Border choice of Frittatas and potato pancakes.

The late-riser menu includes a South of the Border choice of Frittatas and potato pancakes.

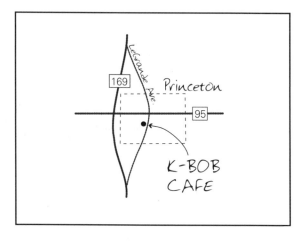

109 LaGrande Ave. S., Princeton, MN 55371
Hours: Mon - Fri 5 a.m. - 8 p.m.
       Sat - Sun 5 a.m. - 2 p.m.
Breakfast served all day
Children's menu
Credit cards: V, MC, D, AE
Phone: 763-389-1361

RICE

FAMILY RESTAURANT

Country Inn Family Restaurant

Rick and Sandy Karasch are the hosts for the Country Inn which is conveniently located in Rice, a smallish village to the north of St. Cloud.

The restaurant is a little oasis for the traveler en route to or from their resort or camp.

With breakfast served all day and a menu that takes in biscuits and gravy, omelettes and hotcakes, the cafe fills up quickly.

Lunch includes burgers and a club sandwich selection with specials listed on their announcement board. Dinners include steak, fish, pork and varied daily choices. Completing the list are salads, chili, famous chicken dumpling soup, rolls and homemade pies.

The restaurant is a little oasis for the traveler enroute to or from their resort or camp.

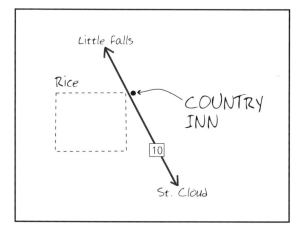

2378 Pine Rd. N.W., Rice MN 56367

Hours: Mon - Thurs 6 a.m. - 9:30p.m.,
Fri - Sat 6 a.m. - 10 p.m.
Sun 7 a.m. - 9:30 p.m.
Call for Holiday and Winter hours

Breakfast served all day

Children's menu

Smoking in designated area

Credit cards: V, MC, D

Phone: 320-393-2066

R

RUSH CITY

ON THE NATIONAL REGISTER OF HISTORIC SITES

The Grant House Hotel & Eatery

Registered nationally as a historic site, the Grant House conveys a feeling of antiquity. The ambiance resembles a farm house kitchen with vintage chairs and tables offering a sense of real homeyness.

The Eatery has a reputation for their substantial portions. Breakfasts begin with homemade rolls and muffins, leading to variety of three-egg omelettes, malted waffles and blueberry pancakes.

The lunch selection of sandwiches is lengthy with some nice variations. The Swedish Patty Melt and Haystack Ham and Cheese are popular choices and all sandwiches are served with a choice of freshly baked breads.

There are also baskets and burgers available with a 6 oz. buffalo burger, a distinctive choice. Dinners include prime rib, walleye, meat loaf, cod and BBQ ribs. For smaller appetites, there is a lite side menu served from 11:30 a.m. to closing.

Their Sunday dinners are a specialty with baked turkey, country baked chicken and baked ham added to the menu. Dinners include a salad bar and a dessert.

The Swedish patty melt and Haystack Ham and Cheese are popular choices.

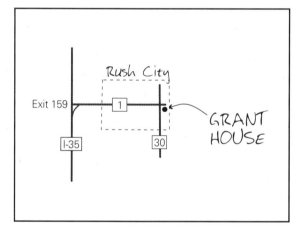

80 W. 4th St., Rush City, MN 55069

Hours: Mon - Tues 6 a.m. - 2 p.m.
          Wed - Thurs 6 a.m. - 8 p.m.
          Fri - Sat 6 a.m. - 9 p.m.
          Sun 7 a.m. - 6:30 p.m.
          Closed Holidays

Children's menu

Smoking in designated area

Credit cards accepted

Phone: 320-358-3661

SCHROEDER

Cross River Cafe

The Cross River Cafe is located in the heart of Schroeder on Minnesota's unique North Shore. The city itself is approximately 32 miles south of Grand Marais on Highway 61.

Their menu offers a wide selection beginning with breakfast which includes made-from-scratch pastries and a caramel roll voted the best on the North Shore. Lunch includes Reubens (or Rachels) and their special Cross River Burger Basket, a California bacon double cheeseburger. The dinner entrees include steak, fish and chicken dishes. The cafe also offers daily specials and homemade rolls, pies and cookies.

The decor features a Minnesota wildlife theme with local photography and floral crafts.

Lunch includes Reubens (or Rachels) and their special Cross River Burger Basket, a California bacon double cheeseburger.

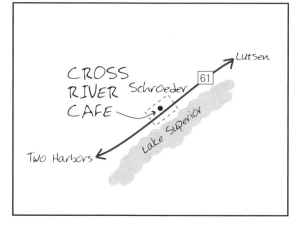

Hwy 61, Schroeder, MN 55613
Hours: Daily 6 a.m. - 9 p.m. Summer/Fall
        Daily 6 a.m. - 8 p.m. Winter/Spring
Phone: 218-663-7208

TAYLORS FALLS

The Drive-In Restaurant

As the Drive-In boasts, the special nature of this unique dining experience is to provide customers with real quality and a special commitment to service recalled from the past.

With takeout dining in the picnic area or car, the Drive-In offers traditional favorites such as hand-packed burgers, onion straws and cross-track fries. Specialities include a hot ham and Swiss, veggie sub, roast beef and cheese or a shrimp, fish and Mexican basket. Fountain drinks include home-made root beer or real cherry coke.

For the youngsters, there is a kid's menu, coupons for mini golf and World's Smallest Sundae.

The Drive-In offers traditional favorites such as hand-packed burgers, onion straws and cross-track fries.

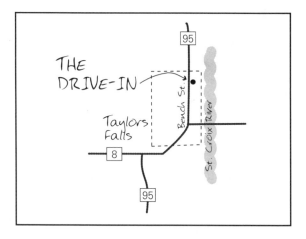

572 Bench St., Taylors Falls, MN 55084-1126
Hours: Memorial Day through Labor Day
            Daily 11 a.m. - 10 p.m.
Cash or check only
For take out: 651-465-7831
Phone: 800-998-4448

TAYLORS FALLS

Rocky River Bakery

A must stop in the area. All the "goodies" one expects from a bakery plus great sandwiches and soups.

Owners Bill and Beth Hughes, share the duties associated with the bakery's menu. Bill, with 40 years of experience as a baker (beginning with training in the Scandinavian and German tradition), handles the bakery products while Beth creates the deli menu.

In addition to the traditional bakery goods, Bill concentrates on his wonderful breads which attract customers from areas such as Red Wing and Albert Lea. As the breads feature reduced preservatives and are low in salt and sugar, they are sought by those with special dietary needs, yet are wonderful for everyone. Selections include sourdough, wild rice oatmeal, sunflower, multigrain and tomato pesto.

Beth tends the soup menu creating her secret recipe, Wild Rice and Ham, along with split pea, potato and occasional specialty varieties such as red bean and rice. The sandwich board is a "design your own" with a choice of meats (turkey, smoked turkey, ham, roast beef) and cheeses (American, Swiss, Mozzarella and provolone) and any of their breads.

Simply call 651-465-ROLL (651-465-7655) for information or to order ahead.

Their breads include sourdough, wild rice oatmeal, sunflower, multi-grain and tomato pesto.

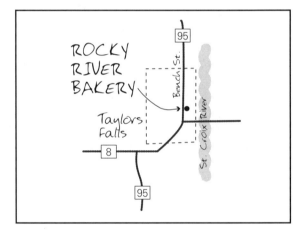

360 Bench St., Taylors Falls, MN 55084
Hours: Daily 7 a.m. - 6 p.m.
        Call for major Holidays
No smoking
Cash or check
Phone: 651-465-7655

TOWER

ERICA'S BAKERY

Erica's Bakery

Certainly a nice station to stop by for a bag of fresh goodies to go, or to sit for a spell at their little counter and enjoy a cup of coffee, with friends (new and old), and a guiltless donut or two.

The bakery, which also supplies neighboring restaurants with their bakery needs, serves up wonderful long johns, bismarcks, bear paws, bars, cheesecakes, elephant ears, eclairs, cinnamon rolls, turnovers, cookies and a gooey butter cake.

A full complement of breads (honey wheat, Synoda, wild rice pecan, Limpa, sourdough, pumpernickel, French, Italian and Swedish Rye), dinner rolls, sandwich buns and muffins are freshly prepared by this busy little shop. Hot pasties are also served during the luncheon hour.

All in all, a very nice refuge in the northwoods of Minnesota.

Serves up wonderful long johns, bismarcks, bear paws, bars, elephant ears, eclairs, cinnamon rolls, turnovers, cookies and a gooey butter cake.

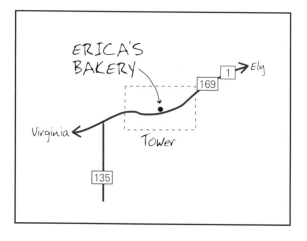

509 Main St. (P.O. Box 360), Tower, MN 55790

Hours: Winter: Mon - Tues 6 a.m. - 2 p.m.
                     Thurs - Fri 6 a.m. - 4:30 p.m.
                     Sat 7 a.m. -12 noon
                     Closed Wed and Sun
             Summer: Mon - Fri 6 - 5 p.m.
                     Sat 6 a.m. - 2 p.m.
                     Closed Sun

No smoking

Phone: 218-753-4705, 888-801-3233

TOWER

TOWER
CAFE

Tower Cafe

Simply one of the nicest little cafes in Minnesota's northwoods area. Located on the north side of highway 169 in Tower, this sparkling cafe brings the woods inside. Do not be deceived by its plain-ish exterior. The restaurant is done in knotty pine with hurricane lamps and both numerous and diverse forest artifacts.

The Tower Cafe has been on 411 Main since 1950, serving both a local and tourist clientele. The cafe does offer a discounted senior menu.

The menu is basic foodstuffs with daily specials such as roast beef, baked ham, baked chicken or roast pork. Naturally, soups and mashed potatoes are homemade. Lunch features a large sandwich menu with a good variety of salad alternatives. Since they are in northern Minnesota, walleye and chili are also on the menu.

*Simply one of the nicest little cafes in
Minnesota's northwoods area.*

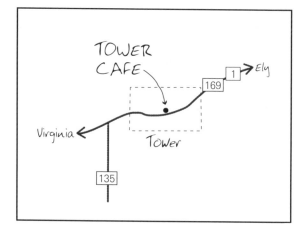

411 Main St., Tower, MN 55790
Hours: Mon - Sat 7 a.m. - 7 p.m.
        Sun 7 a.m. - 3 p.m.
        Open most holidays
Children's menu
Smoking in designated area
Cash only
Phone: 218-753-2710

TWO HARBORS

Betty's Pies

A North Shore distinctive landmark since 1956, Betty's Pies is two miles north of Two Harbors on Highway 61.

This is pure homemade food served in a simple rustic setting warmed by a blue and white color scheme. The cafe is smallish with a short wait as busy times are not terribly unusual. The world famous pies, however, are well worth any delay, or can be ordered ahead with a phone call.

Balancing the homemade pie menu are lunches and dinners with meat, fresh lake Superior trout, vegetarian pastries, soups and sandwiches and delicious breakfasts with homemade muffins and cinnamon rolls.

Nature lends its charm to the cafe's character by affording visitors to a wonderful view of Lake Superior to the East.

*The world famous pies, however, are
well worth any delay, or can be
ordered ahead with a phone call.*

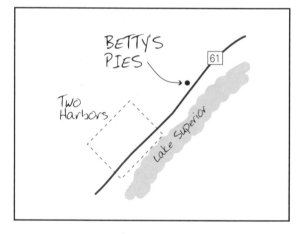

215 E. Hwy 61, Two Harbors, MN 55616
Hours: Daily 8 a.m. - 8 p.m.
            Open Holidays
Breakfast served to 11 a.m.
Children's menu
Credit cards: V, MC
Phone: 218-834-3367, 877-269-7494

TWO HARBORS

Vanilla Bean Bakery & Cafe

The Vanilla Bean is a recommended stop for anyone headed up 61 on Minnesota's North Shore.

Visitors can relax anytime over an espresso or frothy cappuccino and, if so inclined, perhaps an appetizer or a bakery goodie.

For the fortunate who are within striking distance of Two Harbors during meal periods, the Vanilla Bean provides some remarkable variety on the standard offerings. Breakfast includes inch-high oven-baked omelettes, crepes or Swedish pancakes with lingonberries.

Lunchtime selections include wonderful homemade soups, salads with homemade dressing and pasties made fresh daily in the bakery. Breads, such as onion rye or spinach parmesan, are the base for the Bean's unique sandwiches.

Dinners include walleye, shrimp Florentine or, on occasion, a traditional Scandinavian Special.

Fresh, homemade desserts are a specialty of the kitchen.

Breads, such as onion rye or spinach parmesan, are the base for the "Bean's" unique sandwiches.

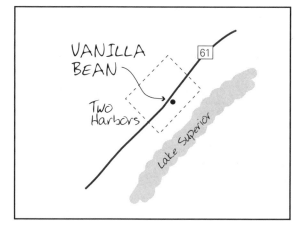

812-7th Ave. (Hwy 61), Two Harbors, MN 55616
Hours: Cafe opens daily at 7 a.m.
           Bakery opens daily at 6 a.m.
No smoking
Credit cards: V, MC, D, AE
Phone: Cafe - 218-834-3714
           Bakery - 218-834-6964

VIRGINIA

Deb's Diner

As the traveler might suspect, genuine Minnesota food is found on the Iron Range in Virginia. Deb's Diner, a favorite meeting and greeting spot, prepares old fashioned home-style meals, all served by a friendly gang whose aim is to put a smile on your face.

The menu is predictable. Customers are not at Deb's for discovery, but for foods that make you feel at home.

Deb's prides itself on homemade soups, chili, hot sandwiches, a Friday night fish fry and specials which are served Monday-Friday until gone.

At breakfast the kitchen rattles out the basic egg and cake favorites and adds a Cowboy or Deb's Super Starter for the big eater.

The atmosphere is clean, bright and comfortable with some homemade crafts for sale which are made by one of the workers.

The breakfast kitchen rattles out basic egg and cake favorites or a Cowboy or Deb's Super Starter for the big eater.

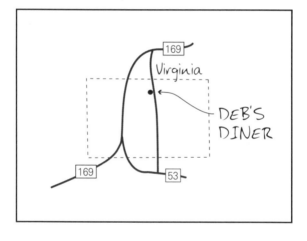

1800 N. 9th Ave., Virginia, MN 55792
Hours: Mon - Thurs 5 a.m. - 7 p.m.
          Fri 5 a.m. - 9 p.m., Sat 5 a.m. - 7 p.m.
          Closed Sundays and Holidays
Breakfast served all day
Tykes menu and senior discount
Smoking in designated area
Cash only
Phone: 218-741-3228

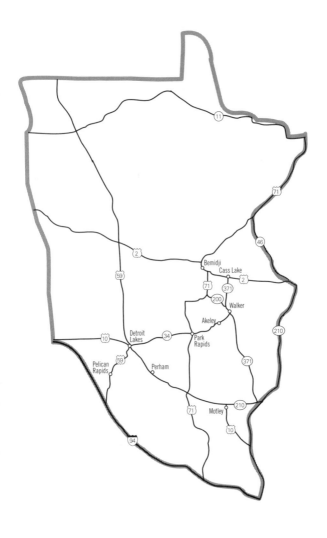

Northwest

AKELEY

Ann's Cafe

Author Ann Spencer will welcome you to her cafe located in Akeley, originally a logging community.

Housed in a 1900s vintage building, the restaurant is one block from the popular Heartland Trail, a paved trail for bicycling, hiking and winter snowmobiling.

Ann's emphasis is on home cooking with home-made buttermilk pancakes, biscuits and gravy featured for breakfast. Sundaes, milk shakes and ice cream are popular items for the tourists.

The atmosphere is relaxed with friendly personal-ized service. Customers are really guests in this unhurried little cafe. There are a few selected antiques and crafts for sale.

Home cooking with homemade buttermilk pancakes, biscuits and gravy featured for breakfast.

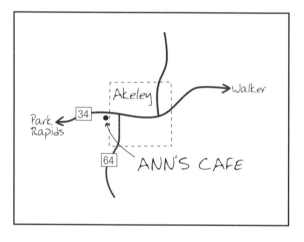

Route 34, Akeley, MN 56433

Hours: Summer: Mon - Sat 7 a.m. - 6 p.m.
Closed Sun and Holidays
Winter: Tues - Sat 8 a.m. - 2 p.m.
Closed Sun, Mon and Holidays

Children portions available

Smoking permitted but not encouraged

Cash only

Phone: 218-652-2988

A

AKELEY

Brauhaus German Restaurant & Lounge

The Brauhaus is a Germanic cookery between Akeley and Nevis in a can't-be-missed location on Highway 34.

Their wonderful food, prepared in the classic style, is served in the traditional setting of Southern Germany.

The casual environment gives way to outgoing and attentive staff attired in German fashions.

Entrees are compelling. Among their European selection the diner will find roasted duck, Euro Goulash, Jagerschnitzel, Schweinehaxe and Sauerbraten. For the less adventuresome, the restaurant provides basket dinners and American invitations of steaks, walleye or ribs. All dinners come with a choice of mashed potatoes, spaetzle or steamed carrots, served with a choice of bread dumplings, sauerkraut or red cabbage and includes sourdough bread or Brotchen.

Off-menu specials may include a plum glazed duck, Atlantic salmon with tarragon sauce, rotisserie pork, buffalo steak or buffalo burgers. You will discover how much there is to traditional German cooking.

The area itself is rich in activities and home to numerous resorts, trails and a variety of sporting opportunities.

Among European selections: roasted duck, Euro Goulash, Jagerschnitzel, Schweinehaxe and Sauerbraten.

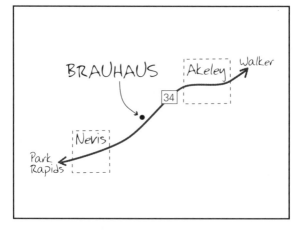

Hwy 34, Akeley, MN 56433

Hours: Spring/Fall: Thurs - Fri 4 - 9 p.m.
              Sat 4 - 10 p.m.
              Sun 12 noon - 9 p.m.
       Summer: Mon - Fri 4 - 9 p.m.
              Sat 4 - 10 p.m.
              Sun 12 noon - 9 p.m.

Children's menu and a smaller portions selections

Smoking in designated area

Reservations accepted for parties of 6 or more

No credit cards

Phone: 218-652-2478

ALEXANDRIA

Downtown Diner

This popular hometown diner is located in one of Minnesota's prime resort and tourist areas, Alexandria Lakes.

Known for excellent fishing, snowmobiling, downhill and crosscountry skiing, golf, summer theatre, riding trails and State Parks, "Alex" as it's often referred to, is a busy and active community.

Nourishing the families of visitors, Joni Aslagson provides simple quality home-style food from her friendly cafe.

Everyday specials are available for both lunch and breakfast. The daily breakfast menu may include two egg omelettes, a Texas toast sandwich or a cinnamon French toast. These choices complement the regular entrees including biscuits and gravy (the #1 seller), blueberry pancakes, or traditional egg and meat dishes which can be ordered with fresh cut American fries.

Lunches and lunch specials vary seasonally. Salads are popular summertime selections with the winter menu tending toward more staple items including the popular scalloped potatoes and ham or homemade beef stew. Specials of the day include Thursday Burger Day (burgers are a "buck") and fish specials on Fridays. Additional daily specials include meat loaf, pork chops, sausage and kraut and a variety of homemade soups. A cup of fresh coffee along side of nice caramel roll is another reason to stop by and enjoy the companionship of this friendly cafe.

*Specials of the day include Thursday
Burger Day (burgers are a "buck")
and fish specials on Fridays.*

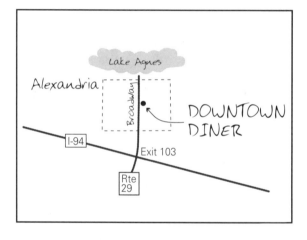

411½ Broadway St., Alexandria, MN 56308

Hours: Mon - Fri 6 a.m. - 3 p.m.
          Sat 6 a.m. - 1 p.m., Sun 7 a.m. - 1 p.m.
          Closed Holidays

Breakfast all day

Children's menu

Smoking in designated area

Cash or check only

Phone: 320-763-1703

BAUDETTE

The Ranch House

The Ranch House

Baudette, a smallish community of 1200, is located on the Rainy River as it flows into the Lake of the Woods. Located in this very popular outdoor paradise, the Ranch House serves 500 to 800 customers daily and over 1000 per day on holiday weekends.

For over 30 years the cafe has been nourishing hungry patrons, the last several under the ownership of Greg Dunrud.

Foods, as might be expected in the fresh and airy northwoods, are served in ample proportions. Pancakes are of the spill-over-the-plate dimensions. If there is a larger 'cake in the state it has yet to be identified. The breakfast menu continues with house specials such as the Logger, Ranchers, or Round Up, with biscuits and gravy served on Sundays. Real hash browns accompany the regular meat and egg entrees.

Lunch choices include super sandwiches with the popular Sod Buster and Western Cheeseburger topping the list. Patty melts, Reubens, the Shore Lunch and a variety of baskets complete the regular lunch menu. Specials are available everyday as is the soup and sandwich creation of the day.

The dinner menu features walleye cooked to order, dry aged steaks and nightly specials. Monday is the all-you-can-eat shrimp, Tuesday fish and chips, on Fridays prime rib and Saturdays BBQ Ribs. A salad bar is available at both lunch and dinner.

If there is room left over the Ranch House will gladly fill it with a piece of their homemade pie.

Pancakes are of the "spill over the plate" dimensions. If there is a larger 'cake in the state it has yet to be identified.

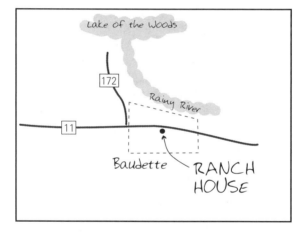

203 W. Main St., Baudette, MN 56623

Hours: Mon - Sat 5:30 a.m. - 10 p.m.
        Sun 6 a.m. - 10 p.m.
        Open Holidays except Thanksgiving and
            Christmas Day

Breakfast served to 11 a.m. daily; 1 p.m. Sun;
        omelettes served any time

Children's menu

Smoking permitted in coffee shop

Credit cards accepted

Phone: 218-634-2420

B

BEMIDJI

Raphael's Bakery & Cafe

Raphael's Bakery & Cafe

Raphael's is one of these wonderful generational eateries which continues to create homemade pastries, breads and assorted bakery delicacies.

Located in Bemidji, the bakery has been a downtown fixture since its beginning in 1950, founded by current proprietor Ray Sweeny's father, Raphael.

The bakery's specialties are breads, angel foods, old fashioned cake donuts and cinnamon rolls. Bread selection is a menu in itself extending from Old World ryes and sourdoughs to whole grain. Two unequaled choices are the Frontier Bread and their Wild Rice Bread, created by Ray's father in 1973.

The cafe offers homemade soups and sandwiches. Soup specials are memorable. Daily choices are wild rice, Scandinavian creamy vegetable, chicken and dumpling or cream of Reuben, with sauerkraut and rye bread croutons. Sandwiches are also a daily special of ham, egg or chicken salad. Customers also enjoy the create-your-own sandwich from a listing of meats and cheeses. Seasonally, homemade chili is another popular menu offering.

*Two unequaled choices are the
Frontier Bread and their Wild Rice
Bread, created by Ray's father in 1973.*

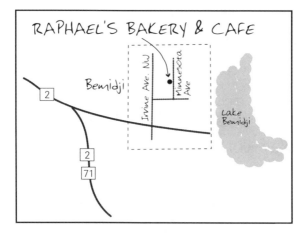

319 Minnesota Ave., Bemidji, MN
Hours: Mon - Fri 6 a.m. - 5:30 p.m.
        Sat 6 a.m. - 2 p.m.
        Closed Sundays and Holidays
No smoking
Cash only
Phone: 218-759-2015

C

CASS LAKE

Canal House Restaurant (Stony Point Resort)

Quarters for the Canal House Restaurant have changed drastically since the cafe first opened in 1972. Then soup and sandwiches were part of a small menu sold from a mobile home. Now the family operated cafe is housed in an impressive northwoods style structure complete with gift shop and patio overlooking the boat harbor and canal.

The area itself draws a large number of tourists based on a reputation of excellent fishing and the many resorts that offer a wide range of family orientated vacation activities. The Chippewa National Forest visitor center, a 1930s log lodge at Norway Beach on Cass Lake, offers hiking opportunities and naturalistic programs for its guests.

As a restaurant, the Canal House concentrates on lunch and dinner with breakfast offered weekends only. Especially popular are the cafe's daily all-you-can eat specials including Wednesday, broasted chicken, Thursday, BBQ ribs and Friday, fish fry. Their sandwich menu harmonizes nicely with the burger choices which can be ordered with a fresh salad bar option.

Dinner selections add walleye, a vegetable, chicken or fettuccine and beef dishes. A lighter meal menu is also provided.

*Dinner selections add walleye,
a vegetable, chicken or fettuccine
and beef dishes.*

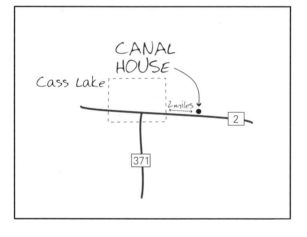

E. Hwy 2, Cass Lake, MN 56633

Hours: Open 5/5 to 9/30
Mon - Fri 11 a.m. - 9 p.m.
Sat 8 a.m. - 10 p.m., Sun 9 a.m. - 9 p.m.

Breakfast served to 11 a.m. - Sat and Sun only

Children's menu

Credit cards accepted

Phone: 218-335-6311

DETROIT LAKES

Main Street Restaurant

Detroit Lakes was originally called simply Detroit. Finding confusion with a Michigan city of the same name, the city fathers added "Lakes" sometime in the late 1800s. The Tamarack National Wildlife Refuge, north of the city, is a favorite destination for birding and wildlife watching.

Satisfying the hunger of their local and tourist clientele, the Main Street is a perfectly pleasant place to sit and enjoy the day.

The meals are big and tasty. This is real home cooking from soup to fresh pies made daily. Their buttermilk pie is a specialty.

A full house enjoys making breakfast decisions while lingering over coffee and chatter. The No. 3 Country Breakfast and No. 6 (Corned Beef Hash and Eggs are the popular choices. As expected, homemade sweet rolls receive a lot of attention. Hot sandwiches, baskets and more baskets accompany the full selection of sandwiches. Pork, chicken, fish, and liver and onions are the dinner favorites, with a lighter side menu as an alternative. The ambience is basically that of a vintage lunchroom.

The meals are big and tasty. This is real home cooking from soup to fresh pies made daily. Their buttermilk pie is a specialty.

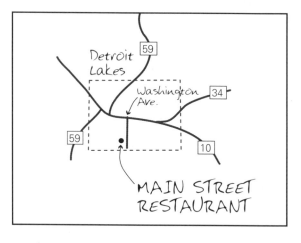

900 Washington Ave., Detroit Lakes, MN 56501
Hours: Mon - Sat 7 a.m. - 5 p.m.
        Sun 8 a.m. - 2 p.m.
        Closed some Holidays
Breakfast all day
Kids Corner menu
Smoking in designated area
Cash only
Phone: 218-847-3344

D

DORSET

Dorset Cafe

Touristy Dorset is located in an area surrounded by lakes and resorts. The popular community offers a variety of small shops and some wonderful dining.

The Dorset Cafe is an especially busy restaurant featuring a wide range of dining options amid a warm and friendly atmosphere. This is a great family restaurant.

For children there is a long list of menu choices while the adults work on steaks, seafood, chicken and pork chops. Some notable selections include the Sizzler Steak prepared Dorset style, broasted pork chops, char-broiled salmon, a variety of shrimp entrees, combo dinners and, of course, walleye. Their signature dishes are BBQ Ribs or a specialty seasoned broasted chicken.

Variety is a cafe theme. On the lite side, salads of choice include either a taco or grilled chicken, and the broiled dinners are accompanied by a seasoned rice. With the general entrée, the diner's choices are au-gratin, hash browns, French fries or the Dorset broasted potato. Homemade soups are always on the menu and the fresh salad bar is available for both lunch and dinner.

Lunches highlight a complete sandwich selection including philly-beef, club, a bacon-chicken melt and either a BBQ or Dorset burger.

*Signature dishes are B-B-Que Ribs or
a specialty seasoned broasted chicken.*

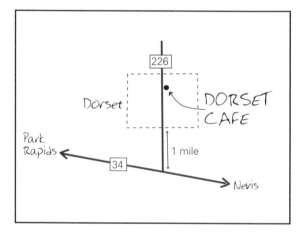

Hwy 226, Park Rapids, MN 56470
Hours: Mon - Sat open at 4:30 p.m.
          Closing time varies
          Sun open at 12 noon
Children's menu
Smoking in designated area
Credit cards accepted
Phone: 218-732-4072

DORSET

La Pasta Italian Eatery/ General Store

Lovers of really good food will enjoy this wonderful, creative cafe. Patrons also enjoy lingering over the annual Dorset Daily Bugle, a really humorous rendition of local and state news.

The charming little community, located next to the Heartland Bike Trail, offers a long list of vacation reasons to consider it a primary destination, not the least of which is the LaPasta/General Store.

Coming from a distant relationship to General George Pickett, owner and chef, Kathy Schmidt uses the images to create her burger selection(s) which include a Robert E. Lee, Mussolini, Franco or Napoleon to name a few. Wraps, subs, Italian specialties and classic sandwiches are also on the lunchtime menu.

The breakfast menu is as extensive as the luncheon list. Especially popular are the Dorset Specialties including a Norwegian Um-lette and Egg in a Cake. All-in-all we are looking at 27 different breakfast choices.

LaPasta is named for the cafes evening food theme. Kathy's specialty sauces are served with a complete variety of traditional Italian pastas, prepared with chicken, sausage, seafood or mushrooms. There are some nice salads on the lighter side menu.

Divided into four separate rooms with an assortment of antique wall decorations, the homey atmosphere is both warm and cozy. Owners, Kathy and Gerald, assure the patron a pleasant dining experience.

Especially popular are the Dorset Specialties including a Norwegian Um-lette and Egg in a Cake.

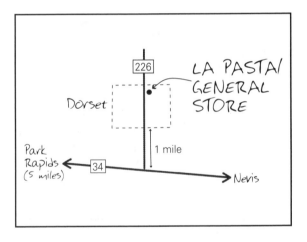

Dorset, Park Rapids, MN 56470
Hours: Daily 7 a.m. - 9 p.m. May - Sept
           (Closed Oct - April)
Breakfast served to 11:30 a.m. (Mon - Sat)
           12 noon (Sun)
Children's menu
Smoking in designated area
Credit cards accepted
Phone: 218-732-0275

M

MOTLEY

Countryside Restaurant

Motley is a north central crossroads community and ideal quarters for a cafe as down-home as the Countryside.

The restaurant is supported by a host of regulars and travelers who find its location perfect for a midtrip break.

Patrons are attracted to the cafe by its large well-cooked meals, all reasonably priced. Homemade cinnamon and caramel rolls start the day sharing orders for their breakfast specials. The friendly and efficient waitstaff reports biscuits and gravy, and their No. 1 (especially low priced eggs, potatoes and toast) are particularly popular. Lunches stress the basics. Hot sandwiches with real mashed potatoes and gravy, burgers, patty melts and a Reuben shape the sandwich menu to accompany homemade soups such as cheese broccoli and California medley.

Dinner entrees are of the meat and potato variety leaning towards chopped steak, pork chops or liver and onions.

For dessert the right choice would be a slice of homemade cream pie.

*Patrons are attracted to the cafe
by its large well-cooked meals,
all reasonably priced.*

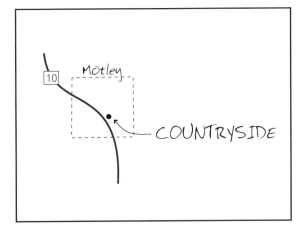

Hwy 10 So., Motley, MN 56466
Hours: 6 a.m. - 10 p.m. everyday
        Open Holidays
Breakfast served all day
Children's menu
Smoking in designated area
Credit cards accepted
Phone: 218-352-6777

NEW YORK MILLS

Eagles Cafe

A not-to-be-missed, family-operated hometown restaurant, the Eagles Cafe is an easy stop along Highway 10.

Jean Gerber, husband Orv, son Tom and wife Julie, have successfully operated their hometown cafe since 1984. Tom handles the major portion of the cooking while Jean and Julie tend the baking side of the business.

Meals are substantial and fresh, from soup to pies, with everything cooked to order.

Breakfast begins with their homemade caramel and cinnamon rolls made fresh everyday, and then leads to a full menu of omelettes, pancakes, meats and French toast.

Lunches consist of a choice between 40 or so sandwich varieties or the "specials" which alternate between 35-40 different entrees. The sandwich board lists their popular Chicken Supreme, French dip and burger assortment while the special could be chow mein, Swiss steak or a hot dish.

There are evening specials as well, including steaks, ham steak, chicken, pork chops or liver and onions. Sundays, the kitchen really goes to work preparing homemade bread and rolls to accompany the from-scratch mashed potatoes and gravy with a baked ham or chicken dinner.

Meals are substantial and fresh, from soup to pies, with everything cooked to order.

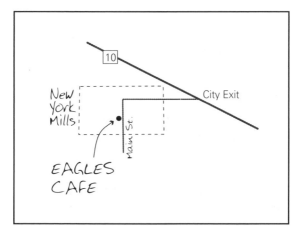

31 North Main St., New York Mills, MN 56567
Hours: Daily 6 a.m. - 8 p.m.
          Closed Major Holidays
Children's menu
Smoking in designated area
Credit Cards: V, MC
Phone: 218-385-2469

PARK RAPIDS

Great Northern Cafe

This home-style Park Rapids eatery inherits its name from the proximity of the old railroad tracks and former train station in the area.

The railroad theme is highlighted by adopting a train-orientated environment and menu choices using compatible descriptions.

Breakfast can begin with either a Great Northern Omelette (basically of the kitchen sink variety), a German omelette, country eggs, 13 Switchman's entrees or biscuits and gravy. Midday ideas include Belly Buster Burgers, a Box Car Hoagie, or Hobo Taco Salad.

The dinner list is composed of the homemade basics with a particular emphasis on their chicken selection.

The real daily special is owner Lance Pritchetts homemade soup. Among the legendary and filling creations are taco, Reuben, potato, chicken dumpling and hamburger pepper.

The real daily special is owner Lance Pritchett's homemade soup. Among the legendary and filling soup creations are taco, Reuben, potato, chicken dumpling and hamburger pepper.

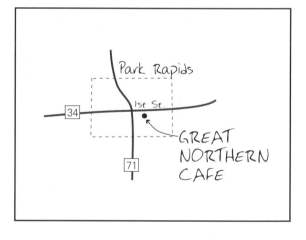

218 E. 1st St., Park Rapids, MN 56470

Hours: Mon - Sat 6 a.m. - 7 p.m.
Sun 6 a.m. - 2 p.m.
Holidays 6 a.m. - 2 p.m. (except Easter, Thanksgiving, and Christmas Day)

Breakfast served until 12 Noon

Children's menu

Smoking in designated area

Cash and check

Phone: 218-732-9565

PARK RAPIDS

Rapid River Logging Camp

Of novel character, the Rapid River Logging Camp is set on the grounds of an early logging camp and sawmill.

Open during the summer, guests should schedule their arrival to coincide with demonstrations of the old steam engine and allow time for short hikes to original landmarks of the logging days.

The authenticity of the experience is evident with their all-you-can-eat meals, served family style, in the camps cook shanty. Breakfast consists of flapjacks and ham and eggs. Lunch is served in a skillet with all-you-can-eat cole slaw, beans and potato salad and dinners all served on metal dishes. The dinner listing includes roast beef, chicken, ham, roast pork or BBQ ribs.

On site the Camp also has a wonderful gift shop with hand crafted items, antiques and artifacts from the logging era.

The authenticity is evident with their all-you-can-eat meals, served family style, in the camps cook shanty.

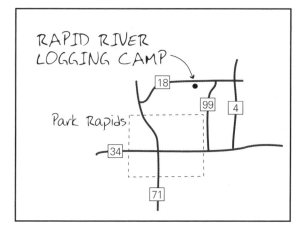

Co. Rd. 18 (Rte. 6 Box 86A), Park Rapids, MN 56470
Hours: Open Memorial Day - Labor Day
          Daily 7:30 a.m. - 9 p.m.
Breakfast served 7:30 until 11 a.m.
Lunch served 12 noon to 3 p.m.
Dinner served 4 p.m. to 9 p.m.
Cash only
Phone: 218-732-3444 (in season)

PARK RAPIDS

Schwarzwald Inn

Jorg Toll is proprietor of the Schwarzwald Inn, a favorite restaurant for townfolk and visitors alike in the touristy area of Park Rapids.

Headquarters for the Itasca State Park, Minnesota's first state park and the origin of the Mississippi, the area is a popular destination for vacationers who enjoy the numerous lakeside family resorts and outdoor activities.

The casual cafe features genuine German specialties and American favorites. Among the entrees are German goulash, baked pork hocks, spaetzle and schnitzel (pork steak). Homemade German bread and homemade soups are served daily. German beers and wines are also available.

Breakfast selections include the usual egg and meat basics and luncheon options are primarily American in character.

The decor is a German alpine motif with pictures, plates, traditional cuckoo clocks and a circling German train. The restaurant's name means *black forest*, the area of Germany from which the Toll family emigrated.

Entrees include German goulash, baked pork hocks, wiener schnitzel and spaetzle. Homemade German bread and homemade soups are served daily.

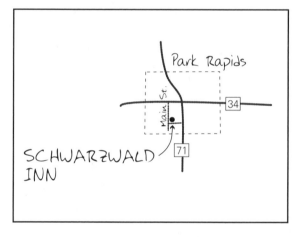

Park Rapids

Main St.

34

SCHWARZWALD INN

71

122 S. Main St., Park Rapids, MN 56470
Hours: Mon - Sun and Holidays 7 a.m. - 9 p.m.
Breakfast served all day
Children's menu
Smoking in designated area
Cash or check
Phone: 218-732-8828

PELICAN RAPIDS

Auntie Ev's
Family Restaurant

Auntie Ev's

The lakes area city of Pelican Rapids in picturesque Otter Tail County is home to Auntie Ev's
Family Restaurant. Timing of the visit may coincide with specialized refurbished antiques for sale.

Good square meals are served in the Cafe's atmosphere of "where friends and family meet." Visitors
are greeted with accommodating tables and booths.

Theirs is not a fancy menu and the kitchen concentrates on the basics. Eggs and meats provide staple
breakfasts with alternatives of pancakes or biscuits
and gravy. Sandwiches served on croissants and
burgers are lunchtime favorites with dinner choices
of fried chicken, hamburger steak, ribs, breaded
cod or jumbo shrimp.

Cafe specials vary daily. Thursdays feature stuffed
pork chops, Friday chicken or pizza, Saturday
walleye or BBQ ribs and a Sunday buffet which
begins at 11 a.m. A fresh salad bar is included with
their all-you-can-eat specials.

For a slightly different spin, their own homemade
pizza, a town favorite, is available for eat-in or
take out.

*A fresh salad bar is included with
their all-you-can-eat specials.*

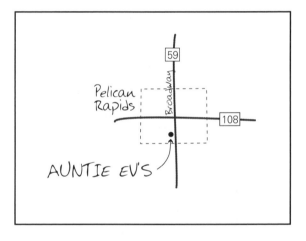

10 S. Broadway, Pelican Rapids, MN 56572

Hours: Winter: Mon - Tues 6 a.m. - 5 p.m.
                Wed - Sun 6 a.m. - 5 p.m.
         Summer: Mon - Sat 6 a.m. - 8 p.m.
                Sun 8 a.m. - 8 p.m.
         Open Holidays except Thanksgiving
                and Christmas

Breakfast served all day

Children's menu

Smoking in designated area

Cash only

Phone: 218-863-5305

PELICAN RAPIDS

The Rapids Cafe

Friendly, touristy Pelican Rapids is close to resorts, scenic byways and a variety of both summer and winter activities. It is also the gateway to Maplewood State Park.

Since 1983 The Rapids Cafe has been creating family style meals for the community and visitors. The attraction is quality of food, reasonable prices and generous portions. With friendly service the atmosphere is relaxed, in the owners term "casual family."

In terms of foods, the Rapids Cafe customers are not here for discovery. Meals are basic fare with all the care of homemade goodness. Omelettes, 'cakes and egg combinations start the day. Lunches are standard sandwiches which can be ordered as a basket and the hot sandwich varieties are served with real mashed potatoes and homemade gravy. Homemade soup is available for lunch or dinner, with their chicken dumpling a creation of regional notoriety. Dinner choices include chicken strips, fish and batter and a hamburger steak. Desserts feature homemade pastries with a changing variety.

Homemade soup is available for lunch or dinner, with their chicken dumpling a creation of regional notoriety.

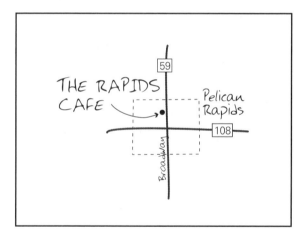

40 N. Broadway, Pelican Rapids, MN 56572
Hours: Mon - Sat 5:30 a.m. - 4 p.m.
        Sun and Holidays 6:30 a.m. - 2 p.m.
Breakfast served all day
Children's and seniors' menu
Full catering available
Smoking in designated area
No credit cards
Phone: 218-863-1726

P

PERHAM

Lakes Cafe

Lakes Cafe

Perham's busy home-style cafe is called the Lakes. All American as possible, the eatery's popularity results from good food with reasonable prices.

There are five assorted breakfast specials at very low prices available from 5:30 a.m. to 11:00 a.m. Homemade rolls and muffins are made fresh every-day. Regular choices include a blend of the basics. Egg dishes can be ordered with Polish sausage or corned beef hash and omelettes are available. Specialty sandwiches, burgers, baskets, melts and hot sandwiches (full and ½ order) are favorites from the luncheon selections. Soups are homemade.

Dinners are of the established variety with steaks, chicken and pork served with soup or salad, choice of potato and toast. From 5 p.m. until 8 p.m. dinners come with a small sundae. A specialty of the house is their ½ pound buffalo steak.

The Lakes Cafe also has a nicely priced pie and coffee special.

Perham is an easy on-and-off from the popular northwest route of Highway 10 with the Lakes Cafe easily spotted on the north side of the city's main street.

All American as possible, the eatery's popularity results from good food with reasonable prices.

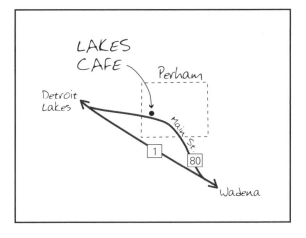

136 W. Main St., Perham, MN 56573
Hours: Mon - Sat 5:30 a.m. - 9 p.m.
 Sun and Holidays 5:30 a.m. - 2 p.m.
Breakfast served all day
Children's menu
Smoking in designated area
Credit cards accepted
Phone: 218-346-5920

PERHAM

The Station House

Perham, located along Highway 10, is a wonderful little town full of interesting shops on main street.

The Station House, constructed in March 1998, has been a popular dining addition to the area. Banquet facilities and a unique gift shop are located on site.

Attention to detail and quality is assured by owners Betty and Don Kennedy, who designed the restaurant's railroad theme and direct the cafe's operation.

With their aggressive menu, the restaurant has a selection for every palate. Farm 'cakes, the German Farmer and Belgian Waffles are a few of the unusual breakfast choices. Sandwich alternatives include their Monte Cristo, Poor Boy Deli and Box Car Chili size. Clam strips, fried chicken, cabbage rolls and steaks are special dinner entrees.

Their wonderful dessert menu presents choices of sundaes, cheesecakes, bread pudding and pies.

Farm 'cakes, the German Farmer and Belgian Waffles are a few of the unusual breakfast choices.

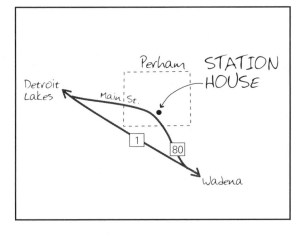

103 E. Main St., Perham, MN 56573
Hours: Daily 7 a.m. - 9 p.m.
Breakfast served to 2 p.m.
Children's and seniors' menu
Smoking in designated area
Credit cards accepted
Phone: 218-348-7181

W

WALKER

The Outdoorsman Cafe

A legend in its own time, the Outdoorsman was the subject of a photograph by William Allard which appeared in the September 1992 issue of the National Geographic.

Owners Guy and Joanie LaFontaine have, since acquiring the cafe in 1985, continued the restaurant's heritage of terrific home-style food and community social forum. The LaFontaines describe the cafe's unique character as "a dynamic marketplace where people barter stories in lieu of material goods." The cafe has become a cornerstone of Walker for local and visitors alike.

The menu begins with a nice assortment of breakfast foods including three egg omelettes, giant buttermilk pancakes and reasonably priced combos with coffee included. Hash browns are from scratch. Since we are in that kind of territory, there is a walleye sandwich on the lunchboard and a walleye fillet for dinner. Club house, BLT's, melts and baked ham are sandwich features, with liver and onions, beef and pork tenderloin among the dinner specials. Soups and chilis are naturally homemade.

Since we are in that territory, there is a walleye sandwich on the lunch-board and a walleye fillet for dinner.

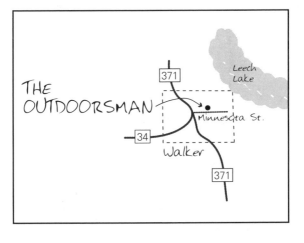

511 Minnesota Ave. W., Walker, MN 56484
Hours: Mon - Sat 6 a.m. - 4 p.m.
            Sun and Holidays 6 a.m. - 12 noon
Breakfast served to 11 a.m.
Children's menu (lunch only)
Smoking in designated area
No credit cards
Phone: 218-547-3310

Southwest

BENSON

Atlantic Junction Limited

Atlantic Junction Limited

The restaurant is an authentic 1889 Pullman Vestibule car which was moved to its present site in downtown Benson in 1934.

Naturally, the atmosphere is old-fashioned, using antiques as decorations, particularly those associated with the railroad which is the cafe's theme.

The menu is tasty with a good selection of entrees and ethnic specials. Breakfast eaters will find a good choice of eggs, meat and 'cake dishes, with the lunches very popular. Their famous meatballs with real mashed potatoes and gravy is served daily and customers will find roast beef, pork and other specials on the menu. Pies, cookies and sweets are homemade.

The menu varies seasonally with fruit dishes and salads in the warmer months and homemade soups and chili during the winter.

Klub (a Norwegian potato dumpling) is a specialty which is served for lunch every Thursday. Sisters Peg Flander and Deb Collins continue their research into the history of the restaurant and invite everyone to stop in for coffee (espresso, lattes and cappuccino) and conversation about the unique diner.

Klub (a Norwegian potato dumpling) is a specialty which is served for lunch every Thursday.

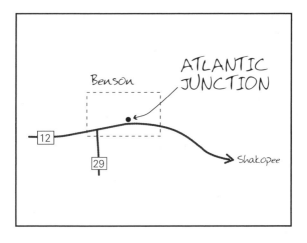

1220 Atlantic Ave. (Hwy 12), Benson, MN 56215

Hours: Mon 6:30 a.m. - 3:30 p.m.
        Tues - Fri 6:30 a.m. - 8 p.m.
        Sat 7:30 a.m. - 3:30 p.m.
        Closed Sundays
        Winter months the restaurant opens at
            7:30 a.m. every day

Children's menu

Smoking in designated area

Cash and credit cards: V, MC, AE

Phone: 320-843-2474

BLUE EARTH

Hamilton's Restaurant

Blue Earth's hometown beanery is Hamilton's Restaurant located on the corner of 7th and Main.

The restaurant's folksy, friendly atmosphere is supported by a staff who keeps the coffee cups full and concentrates on service and detail.

Since Hamilton's has arranged for goodies from an on-site "scratch" bakery, the day begins with a variety of fresh rolls. Naturally, there are caramel and cinnamon taste treats which are supplemented by apple fritters, long johns and cake donuts. Fresh American fries are a nice addition to the traditional breakfast special offered every day with a changing combination of entrees.

For lunch the cafe brings out some excellent specials including chicken and dumplings, meat loaf and a salmon loaf. Among the choices on the sandwich side are 8 oz. hand-pattied burgers, beef commercials (bread, meat, mashed potatoes, gravy) and a nice selection of salads.

The dinner menu concentrates on Hamilton's specialties. Choices include lasagna, chicken, bacon-wrapped chopped steak or a country-fried steak, all served with cole slaw, potato and a dinner roll.

Desserts are not left out. Homemade pies, cookies, bread pudding, malts, shakes, sundaes and even a root beer float are optional for topping off a warm meal.

The restaurant's folksy, friendly atmosphere is supported by a staff who keeps the coffee cups full and concentrates on service and detail.

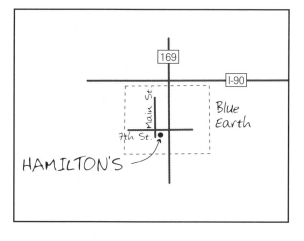

209 S. Main St., Blue Earth, MN 56013

Hours: Daily 6 a.m. - 8 p.m.
          Call for Holiday hours

Breakfast served to 11 a.m.

Children's and seniors' menu

Smoking in designated area

Credit cards accepted

Phone: 507-526-3287

FAIRFAX

The Corner Cafe

When travelers make a special effort to return year after year for good home cooked meals, it's evident a restaurant has a lot going for it. For those whose destinations lie in the direction of the Corner Cafe rewards include the best in freshly prepared meals.

Owner's Morrie and Diane Strain have been in the restaurant business for over 35 years, spending the last 16 developing The Corner Cafe into a popular eatery frequented by local and traveler alike.

Emphasis on fresh, homemade foods account for the cafe's reputation. Meats are delivered from a small market in Mankato (including their breakfast sausage) for use in the restaurant's recipes, while potatoes in every form are made-from-scratch. Nor are foods fancy – a fact reflecting the patron's preferences and the reason visitors regularly return. Do not be misled however by the simple creations as the Corner Cafe's menu offers a large selection.

Breakfasts consist of the basic egg and meat items along with some very good pancakes. Lunchtime selections include 30+ sandwiches, hand-pressed burgers, melts, fish, chicken and Morey's special potato salad. The likeable homemade soups include split pea, beef spaetzle, bean and potato. Among the dinner offerings are roast beef and pork, chicken, chipped beef and chicken-ala-king. Homemade pies are the dessert favorites.

The friendly service and agreeable prices are only added reasons for the Corner Cafe's notoriety.

Travelers make a special effort to return year after year for good home cooked meals.

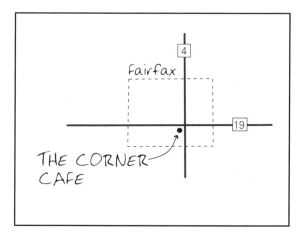

420 E. Lincoln St., Fairfax, MN 55332-3156

Hours: Mon - Sat 7a.m. - 9 p.m. (Winter 8 p.m.)
        Sun 8 a.m. - 8 p.m.
        Closed Thanksgiving, Christmas and
           New Year's

Breakfast served all day

Smoking in designated area

Cash or check

Phone: 507-426-7832

FAIRMONT

The Ranch Family Restaurant

The Ranch's atmosphere begins with their 18-foot detailed sculpture, reminiscent of a 1950s city scene, decorating the entrance to the restaurant. The work was created by artist Michael German.

For 17 years the Ranch has been serving both tourists from I-90 and the local citizenry from a large and diverse menu. Breakfast entrees include a full complement of eggs, meats, pancakes and waffles. Their lunchtime favorites of burgers, salads and such are complemented by their special 40-item salad bar. Dinners are big and tasty featuring steaks, seafood and chicken.

Visitors to Fairmont enjoy water activities on their five inter-connected lakes and demonstrations at the Heritage Acres Agricultural Center.

Their lunchtime favorites of burgers, salads and such are complemented by their special 40-item salad bar.

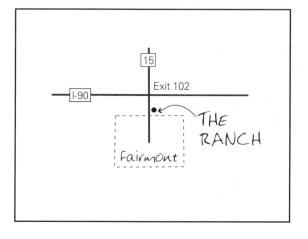

1330 N. State St., Fairmont, MN 56031
Hours: Mon - Sun 6 a.m. - 10 p.m.
           Including Holidays
Breakfast served to 3 p.m.
Children's menu
Smoking in designated area
Credit cards accepted
Phone: 507-235-3044

GRANITE FALLS

The Grinder

Located on busy Highway 212, the Grinder is ideal for a "refresher" after visits to the County Museum or the city park which overlooks the Granite Falls dam.

The cafe is as much an experience as an eatery. Early in the day visitors will find fresh muffins and bagels to enjoy with a variety of coffee associated beverages, while later on the Grinder offers excellent homemade soups and fresh wrap or pita sandwiches. For desserts the choices include ice cream, bars and cookies.

Associated with the cafe are its unique atmosphere and gift shop. Charm results from the fireplace, patio and furnishings, all creating a homey feeling. The assortment of specialty items in the gift shop offers ample opportunity for the browser to shop for all kinds of things including frames, soups, pet and bird supplies and Minnesota foods.

The Grinder offers excellent homemade soups and fresh wrap or pita sandwiches.

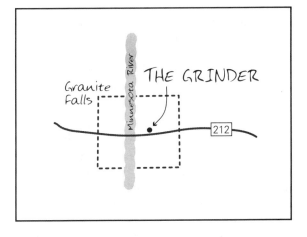

176 E. Hwy 212, Granite Falls, MN 56241

Hours: Mon - Fri 8 a.m. - 5:30 p.m.
        Sat 8 a.m. - 3 p.m.
        Closed Sunday and Holidays

No smoking

Cash, check and credit card: V, MC

Phone: 320-564-4244

HUTCHINSON

Hutch Cafe

Hutch Cafe

Daughters Angela, Maureen and Teresa assumed responsibility of the Hutch from their father in 1993 and continue the standards of fine food and service he began in 1968. Well-schooled in the cafe's enterprise, the girls all started as waitresses later moving into the kitchen as cooks under Dad's tutelage.

The large farm scene painting highlights the "good feeling" of the restaurant's atmosphere and enhances the warmth of the cafe. This is your at-home village cafe where regulars are on a first name basis and often stop in twice a day for coffee and companionship.

The foods are prepared with pure home cooking. Breakfasts are comprised of omelettes, pancakes, potatoes and a variety of meats. Lunches feature a complete selection of burgers, sandwiches, salads and homemade soups. At dinner time the cafe offers homemade specials as well as real turkey dinners, BBQ pork riblets and a very popular broasted chicken. Gravies and mashed potatoes are all homemade.

The McLeod Country Heritage Center is a favorite destination for visitors.

Well-schooled in the cafe's enterprise, the girls all started as waitresses later moving into the kitchen as cooks under Dad's tutelage.

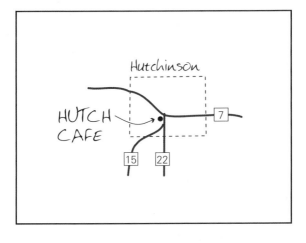

122 S. Main St., Hutchinson, MN 55350

Hours: Mon - Sat 5:45 a.m. - 8 p.m.
       Sun 7 a.m. - 2 p.m.
       Closed Holidays

Breakfast all day

Children's menu

Smoking in designated area

Cash only

Phone: 320-587-2438

JACKSON

The Longhorn Cafe

Jackson, one of Minnesota's prairie communities, lies adjacent to I-90. Fort Belmont, a reconstructed reminder of pioneer life, is a celebrated local attraction.

This family cafe, operated with care and concern by the Kolanders (mother, father, daughter) provides a complete menu of home cooked meals for both the traveler and "hometowner."

A creditably aggressive menu presents a wide variety of choice. Breakfasts are comprised of eggs, meats or 'cakes and such selections. Lunches concentrate on the sandwich side with some interesting variations such as a green olive patty melt, a chicken bacon melt and a "loco" burger.

For adventure, the Longhorn is one of the few restaurants to offer buffalo burgers and a buffalo melt. They also add a South-of-the-Border section to the menu.

Broasted pork chops and broasted chicken accompany the BBQ ribs, beef, shrimp and grilled ham dinner selections. The western theme and environment is well represented by appropriate artifacts.

The Longhorn is one of the few restaurants to offer buffalo burgers and a buffalo melt.

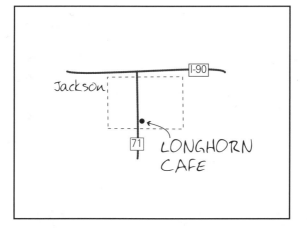

415 S. Hwy 71, Jackson, MN 56143
Hours: Mon - Fri 6 a.m. - 8 p.m.
              Closed Sat, Sun and Holidays
Breakfast served to 11 a.m.
Children's menu
Smoking in designated area
Cash only
Phone: 507-847-5188

LAKE BENTON

The Ridge

Located in the farmland of southwestern Minnesota, Lake Benton offers lake related activities, a season of events at their Opera House (on the National Register of Historic Places), their annual Saddle Horse Holiday and the Hole-in-the-Mountain Prairie Park, a managed preserve of natural grasses, wildflowers and insects.

For dining the city's local home-style restaurant is the Ridge.

Breakfasts consist of the staple eggs and meat combinations, with homemade rolls, their own recipe pancakes and a special egg sandwich.

For lunch and dinner the specialty is beef. Owners and operations of the Ridge, Jerry and Shelly DeLaney are also "ranchers." Raising their own registered polled herefords, the herd is a resource for the dinner table accounting for the wonderful hamburgers and steaks. There are daily specials such as goulash, a tator tot casserole, or Shelly's secret recipe chicken hot dish. Naturally, there is always a beef dinner available. These all go nicely with the homemade potatoes and gravy.

Soups including beef stew, chicken noodle and chili are all homemade. On the dessert side, ice cream treats are a nice mealtime complement.

Daily specials such as goulash, a tator tot casserole, or Shelly's secret recipe chicken hot dish.

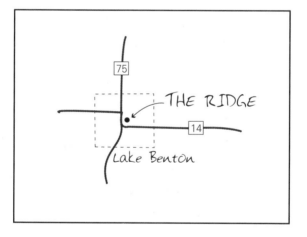

311 N. Center St. (P.O. Box 172)
    Lake Benton, MN 56149

Hours: Seasonal - March 1 to November 1
    Mon - Fri 6 a.m. - 10 p.m.
    Sat 7 a.m. - 10 p.m., Sun 11 a.m. - 10 p.m.

Cash only

Smoking in designated area

Phone: 507-368-9308

LITCHFIELD

Main Street Cafe

Main Street Cafe

The Main Street Cafe is nestled amid buildings of 1870s and 1880s construction in historic downtown Litchfield.

A virtual pictorial history of the community, the cafe walls feature an extensive photographic display of Litchfield's development. It's not unusual, at all, to observe customers roaming through the restaurant to view these wonderful images.

The cafe itself is home-style territory. Known for its variety of breakfast choices, it features classic skillets, including owner Ron Markovich's potato skillet, cinnamon rolls baked fresh daily and gourmet pancakes from an 1800s Pennsylvania Dutch recipe. For lunch, the cafe turns over to daily specials of meat, real mashed potatoes and vegetables, with sandwiches and burgers also available. The Bleu 89'ers and Ripley Sinker are favorite burgers all of which are all hand-pattied.

There have not been many changes to the Main Street Cafe over the years, and it continues to be a popular choice for breakfast and lunch.

*The Bleu 89'ers and Ripley Sinker
are favorites from the burger side
of the menu.*

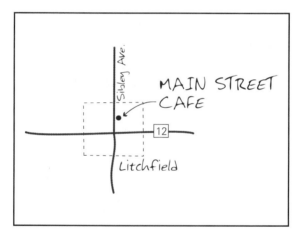

226 N. Sibley Ave., Litchfield, MN 55355
Hours: Mon - Fri 6 a.m. - 4 p.m.
           Sat 6 a.m. - 2 p.m., Sun 7 a.m. - 2 p.m.
Breakfast anytime
Children's menu
Smoking in designated area
Cash only
Phone: 320-693-9067

LITCHFIELD

Parkview Lunch

Across from Central Park in downtown Litchfield, the Parkview lunch is handy for visitors and its local clientele. A fixture, the cafe, with some changes, has been in place for over 50 years.

The '50s style burger shop features great burgers and real mashed potatoes. Malts are still served in the malt tin. The menu offers daily lunch and dinner specials as well as a children's menu. The Parkview kitchen stresses the basics including homemade pies and desserts.

The site is close to the Gar Hale Museum, dedicated to civil war momentos, one of a few remaining museums of this type in the United States.

The '50s style burger shop features great burgers and real mashed potatoes.

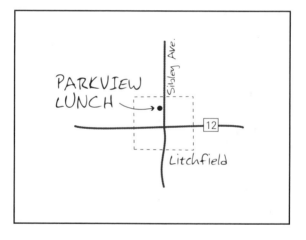

311 Sibley Ave. N., Litchfield, MN 55355
Hours: Mon - Fri 6 a.m. - 8 p.m.
         Sat 7 a.m. - 8 p.m.
         Closed Sundays and Holidays
Breakfast served to 11 a.m.
Children's menu
Smoking in designated area
Cash only
Phone: 320-693-8168

LUVERNE

Blue Mound Inn

From its vantage point, the Inn with 13 picture windows offers wonderful panoramic views of the Blue Mounds (Sioux Quartzite rock formations) and the surrounding countryside.

Foods on the buffet are all homemade from the Inn's kitchen. The presentation includes a variety of the traditional buffet type items. Entrees of meat, fish and chicken are complemented by an assortment of vegetables. The Inn's specials are "turkey on the rock," homemade salads and home-made desserts.

In addition to their gift shop area, the Inn has, on-site, a wayside chapel which is used for weddings and quiet reflection. Their gift shop has items including blue delft glassware.

Specials are "turkey on the rock," homemade salads and desserts.

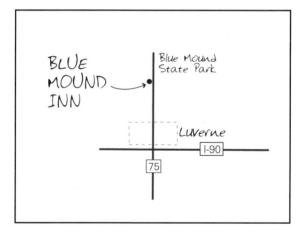

Rte. 1 Box 32A Luverne, MN 56156
Hours: Tues - Sat 5 a.m. - 9 p.m.
        Sun 11a.m. - 8 p.m.
        Closed Mon
        Closed Christmas Eve, Christmas Day
        Call ahead for seasonal hours
Children's menu
Smoking in designated area
Cash only (checks with I.D.)
Phone: 507-283-8364 / 507-283-2718

MANKATO

Stoney's

Stoney's

Described by general manager and host Ray Schwegman as casually upscale, the restaurant features the finest in quality and service.

Not a large facility with the atrium area seating approximately 40 and a total capacity of 100, atmosphere is created by soft colors accentuated by red tablecloths and white linen napkins.

Noted for it's fine food, the luncheon selections feature a variety of appetizers including their signature Baked Coquille Gratinee, followed by a main course menu which includes sandwiches, burgers, pasta and salads. Their soups and pasta selections are all homemade. Among the house specialties are a favored beef strognaoff, beer-battered walleye and Ray's Hot Turkey Salad as featured in the Taste Section of the *Minneapolis Star Tribune*.

Dinners include the enhanced selection of appetizers and expanded pasta, seafood and broiler selections with taste tempting monthly features. The restaurant also specializes in serving Black Angus cuts of beef and has received awards for the best steaks in the Mankato area. Entrees are also served with their noted, and not-to-be missed, house breads prepared by their own baker, from Stoney's special recipe.

Stoney's has established a wide reputation for their specialty deserts which include the Rhubarb Crisp, Fresh Baked Bread Pudding with butterscotch sauce and the special lemon ice.

Luncheon selections feature a variety of appetizers including their signature Baked Coquille Gratinee.

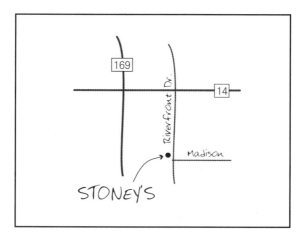

900 N. Riverfront Dr., Mankato, MN 56001
Hours: 11 a.m. - 4 p.m. Lunch
        4 - 10 p.m. Dinner
        Closed - Thanksgiving, Christmas
Full bar service
Smoking in designated area
Credit cards accepted
Phone: 507-387-4813

MARSHALL

Mike's Cafe

The hungry tourist soon discovers Marshall's popular main street eatery, Mike's Cafe. Since 1946 the cafe has been easy to identify by its large neon sign just east of downtown.

At Mike's something homemade is always cooking. As the day begins, customers are greeted by a tempting arrangement of muffins, pecan rolls and cinnamon rolls placed near the cafe's entrance. Egg and meat dishes served with real hash browns are customer favorites.

Mike's big lunchtime seller is the beef commercial (bread, meat, mashed potatoes, gravy) served with real mashed potatoes and gravy. Burgers, sandwiches and salads are additional menu choices. Dinners, fish, chicken and beef entrees are homecooked, topped off with home baked pies and desserts.

Marshall is also the site of Southwestern State University which attracts tourists to its planetarium and Natural History Museum.

Mike's big lunchtime seller is the beef commercial served with real mashed potatoes and gravy.

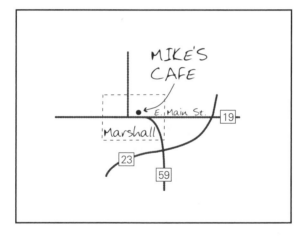

203 E. College Dr., Marshall, MN 56258
Hours: Mon - Sun 6 a.m. - 9 p.m.
Closed Holidays
Breakfast is served all day
Children's menu
Smoking in designated area
Cash only
Phone: 507- 523-5477

MONTEVIDEO

VALENTINO'S

Valentino's Restaurant

Picturesque and historic Montevideo is located in the Minnesota River Valley. Named after the capital of Uruguay, the city's downtown plaza bears the name of the country's liberator.

Visitors in search of history head for the Chippewa City Pioneer Village while others enjoy a stroll or light walk in the city's three parks along the Chippewa River.

In the center of Montevideo, Gabe and Eloise have opened their home-style restaurant, Valentino's.

Artwork of a local craftsman decorates the walls and the use of refinished furniture gives the cafe a cozy and warm feeling. Handmade shelves and unique woodworking by Gabe, as well as antiques and collectables, are attractions.

Made-from-scratch soups, salads, homemade pies, desserts and rolls highlight the menu's basic selections. Breakfasts are popular with a full array of eggs, omelettes and homemade pastries available. Daily specials are offered for the lunchtime appetite and sandwiches are prepared on European style buns. Sunday dinners are a Valentino's specialty.

Daily specials are offered for the lunchtime appetite and sandwiches are prepared on European style buns.

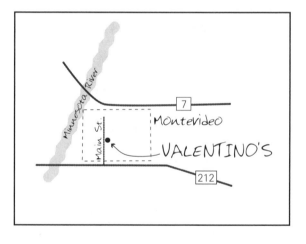

110 S. 1st St., Montevideo, MN 56265
Hours: Mon - Wed, Fri 6 a.m. - 5 p.m.
         Thurs 6 a.m. - 7 p.m.
         Sat 7 a.m. - 3 p.m., Sun 8 a.m. - 2 p.m.
         Closed Holidays
Breakfast served to 11 a.m.
Smoking in designated area
Cash, checks and credit cards: V, MC
Phone: 320-269-5106

NEW ULM

Veigel's Kaiserhoff

Veigel's Kaiserhoff

The cornerstone for dining in the community of New Ulm is Veigel's Kaiserhoff. For 60 years the renowned establishment has been serving steaks, seafood, German dishes and their legendary BBQ ribs. A predominantly wood theme provides warmth for the restaurant's Bavarian atmosphere.

The German menu features sauerkraut balls, wiener schnitzel, bratwurst and a wonderful host of Germanic specialties. The entrée of distinction is the BBQ ribs. Over the years Don Veigel estimated the Keiserhoff has prepared three million pounds of this famous dish served with fried potatoes and onions.

This New Ulm area is rich in Old World charm. With festivals and beautiful homes dating to the 1800s, and shops specializing in German imports, including cuckoo clocks, the atmosphere is distinctively Old World.

A popular nearby diversion is the Harkins Store. The 1800s vintage general store, stocked with goods of the era, is a state historic site.

The German menu features sauerkraut balls, wiener schnitzel, bratwurst and a wonderful host of Germanic specialties.

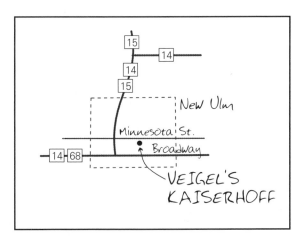

221 N. Minnesota St., New Ulm, MN 56073

Hours: Mon - Fri 11 a.m. - 9:30 p.m.
            Sat 11 a.m. - 10 p.m.
            Sun 11 a.m. - 9:30 p.m.
            Closed Christmas Eve and Christmas

Children's menu

Smoking in designated area

Credit cards: V, MC, D

Phone: 507-359-2071

N

NEW ULM

Ulmer Cafe

The Ulmer's location is matchless. Located in the center of downtown New Ulm, with its endless variety of shopping experiences, the cafe provides the perfect spot for refreshment or to start the shopping day.

Basically, the Ulmer is your old fashioned family restaurant serving homemade food with a German influence.

Breakfast choices begin with a Features section including a specially low priced Herb's Special, then a selection of omelettes and homemade hash browns. For lunch, and a sense of daring, sandwiches such as an Octoberfest, Summer Sausage, Landjaeger are available, or from the burgers side, a Bud, Bavarian or Ulmer are certainly distinctive choices.

From 11 a.m. - 2 p.m. the Ulmer serves some wonderful Daily Dinner Specials. Soup, Dave's Chili, a German Special, beef commercial (bread, meat, mashed potatoes, gravy) and chicken drummies are among the available. Mashed potatoes are homemade. Salads are also on the menu.

Sundaes, pies and an Apple Kuchen appear on the dessert list.

Visitors will enjoy the city of "charm and tradition" with its clearly evident German heritage.

Basically, the Ulmer is your old fashioned family restaurant serving homemade food with a German influence.

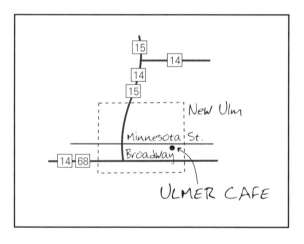

ULMER CAFE

115 N. Minnesota St., New Ulm, MN 56073
Hours: Mon - Fri 5:30 a.m. - 4 p.m.
            Sat 5:30 a.m. - 2 p.m., Sun 8 a.m. - 1 p.m.
            Closed Holidays
Breakfast served to 11 a.m.
Children's menu
Smoking in designated area
No credit cards
Phone: 507-354-8122

OLIVIA

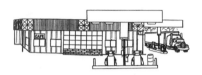

Chatterbox Cafe

Though Garrison Keiller's Chatterbox Cafe is in
Lake Wobegon, the real Chatterbox has been in
Olivia for the last 18 years.

This is a busy restaurant where tourists, sheriffs
and country folk sit comfortably side by side.
Owners Paul and Diane Ager describe their food
as "nothing fancy - just plain home cooking."
That simple philosophy has translated into the
cafes popularity.

There is a wide range of basics on the menu, all
attractively priced. Egg combinations, omelettes,
French toast, pancakes and some nice sized homemade caramel and cinnamon rolls start the day.

The lunch section also has a large list of choices.
Burgers (all hand-pattied ground beef), sandwiches
and croissants, melts, homemade soups and salads
will accommodate every appetite. The dinner list
includes chicken, seafood, pork and beef entrees,
all served with real mashed potatoes.

Homemade pies and cakes are dessert specialties.

This is a busy restaurant where tourists, sheriffs and country folk sit comfortably side by side.

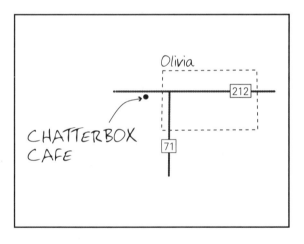

2626 W. Lincoln Ave. (South side of 71/212),
        Olivia, MN 56277
Hours: Mon - Fri 5:30 a.m. - 9 p.m.
        Sat 6:30 a.m. - 3 p.m.
        Sun 7 a.m. - 1:30 p.m.
        Closed Holidays
Breakfast served anytime
Children's menu
Smoking in designated area
Credit cards: V, MC, D
Phone: 320-523-5384

PIPESTONE

**THE
HISTORIC
CALUMET
INN**

The Calumet Inn

Pine dining. Historic setting. Intriguing menu. These elements are all found at the Calumet Inn.

The Inn is in a building constructed in 1888, primarily of reddish Sioux quartzite building stone taken from quarries at Pipestone. The Inn was named to the National Register of Historic sites in 1975.

Entering the dining room is to move to a time gone by as crystal, linen, dark wood and chandeliers convey a feeling of elegance and history.

The distinctive ambiance gives way to a creative and exceptional menu. Morning meals include omelettes - Cajun and Mexican, a Denver skillet or a special French toast. Noon specials are interesting and varied. Regular entrees include a turkey club croissant and Italian veggie sandwich. Dinner selection is made from steak, pasta, stirfry and special seafood main courses. Homemade chicken wild rice soup is available for both lunch and dinner.

As the location for the Pipestone National Monument, Pipestone itself is a prominent site of Indian History.

*Morning meals include omelettes -
Cajun and Mexican, a Denver skillet
or a special French toast.*

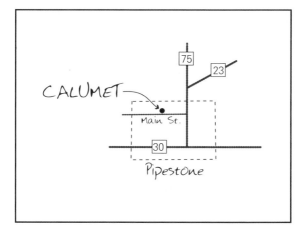

104 W. Main St., Pipestone, MN 56164

Hours: Mon - Thurs 7:30 a.m. - 9 p.m.
Fri - Sat 7:30 a.m. - 10 p.m.
Sun 7:30 a.m. - 8 p.m. (winter), 9 p.m. (summer)
Holidays 7:30 a.m. - 4 p.m., Closed Christmas
Easter and Thanksgiving Buffets 10-2

Breakfast served to 11 a.m.

Children's menu

Dining room smoke free

Lounge smoking permitted (dining service provided)

Credit cards accepted

Phone: 507-825-5871, 800-535-7610

P

PIPESTONE

Lange's Cafe

"Where old friends meet" is the slogan for this 43-year-old Pipestone landmark which is open 24 hours, 7 days a week.

Lange's is precisely the sort of eatery travelers seek in the way of a heartland cafe. Everything is baked from scratch. Donuts, rolls, cakes, cookies, caramel and cinnamon rolls and 27 varieties of pies. Lange's even makes its own premium ice cream.

Though constantly requested, owner Steve Lange, son of one of the founding Lange brothers, refuses to part with the recipes for their homemade pies, soups or their thick hand-sliced bacon.

A four-page menu of breakfast, lunch and evening selections cover all food groups with an unusually wide variety.

Lange's also reflects the nearby National Monument at Pipestone by use of natural artifacts and the famous Peace Pipe in the cafe's decor.

This 43 year old Pipestone landmark is a 24 hour, 7 days a week cafe.

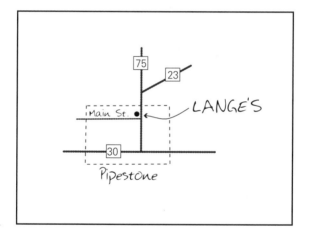

110-8th Ave. S.E., Pipestone, MN 56164
Hours: Open 24 hours, Daily
Breakfast served 24 hours a day
Seniors' menu
Credit cards accepted
Phone: 507-825-4488

REDWOOD FALLS

The Family Food Gallery

The community's scenic Alexander Ramsey Park, along the Redwood River, is a large wooded acreage with waterfalls and hiking paths to explore.

Redwood Falls is also the site of one of the state's busiest home-style cafes. Everyone hungry for breakfast or lunch heads to the Family Food Gallery. Not given to a particular theme or character, comfort is taken from friendly folks enjoying coffee and cribbage or solving the problems of the day.

Good homecooked food as well as delectable meals at reasonable prices are both reasons for the cafe's appeal and popularity.

Food stuffs are not fancy. Eggs and 'cakes for breakfast, including outstanding omelettes and scrambleds. Homemade soups, daily specials and generous beef, turkey and pork commercials (bread, meat, mashed potatoes, gravy) for lunch. Genuine foods that are really quite good.

Good homecooked food at reasonable prices are both reasons for the cafe's appeal and popularity.

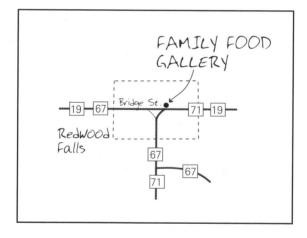

805 E. Bridge St., Redwood Falls, MN 56283
Hours: 6 a.m. - 2 p.m. Daily
Breakfast served all day
Children's menu
Smoking in designated area
Credit cards accepted
Phone: 507-637-5705

ST. JAMES

Hometown Family Restaurant

Hometown Family Restaurant

For some 20 years now the Hometown has been generating real family style meals. Conveniently located, St. James is on Highway 60, a major route from I-90 through Mankato to the Twin Cities.

The restaurant has a complete list of selections. Starting the day, their Skillet Breakfast has become a favorite with a recipe of eggs, meat, hash browns, onions and green pepper covered with cheese. Homemade cinnamon rolls are made fresh daily. French toast and pancakes are popular local choices.

Lunch specials are offered daily. The hot dishes (tuna, chicken and tator tot) are filling temptations. A homemade soup special is on the menu every-day. Among the possibilities are chicken noodle, bean, vegetable beef or hamburger vegetable.

Dinner choices include baked pork chops, meat balls, hamburger steak with fried onions, breaded fish, baked ham or chicken and their popular BBQ ribs. Lunch and dinners are finished with home-made pie or cake.

The atmosphere is bright and fresh with prompt friendly service.

The hot dishes - tuna, chicken and tator tot - are filling temptations.

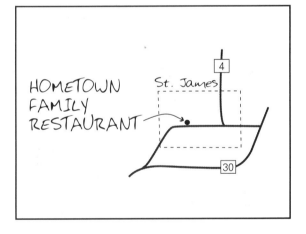

423-1st Ave. S., St. James, MN 56081

Hours: Mon - Fri 6 a.m. - 8 p.m.
Sat 6:30 a.m. - 8 p.m.
Sun 6:30 a.m. - 2 p.m.
Open most Holidays 7 a.m. - 2 p.m.

Breakfast served all day

Children's menu

Smoking in designated area

Cash or check only

Phone: 507-375-4955

ST. PETER

Ooodles Cafe

Ooodles is exactly what one expects in a home-style, hometown cafe – fine people, fine service and the quality recognized in home cooked meals.

Their breakfast specials, coffee included, are attractively priced, offering a choice of four combinations, with homemade pecan or cinnamon rolls always available. The comprehensive menu includes skillets, tator and eggs, biscuits and gravy, steak and eggs, the Ooodles omelette, pancakes or French toast. Naturally, the home fries and hash browns are prepared with fresh potatoes.

Lunchtime specials include soup (homemade) and sandwiches, hand-pattied burgers, baskets, beef commercials (bread, meat, mashed potatoes, gravy) and a turkey or beef fritter sandwich.

All-you-can-eat evening specials vary daily and include a Friday fish fry, Thursday BBQ ribs, Wednesday spaghetti and Tuesday broasted chicken.

Evidencing the quality of food is their daily service to three local daycare centers, as well as serving meals to the homebound. In an "Andy of Mayberry" sort of fashion Ooodles also serves three meals a day to those in the city's "house of detention."

Anyone stopping by midmorning will catch the action as the 10:00 a.m. coffee club (a composition of businessmen of all distinctions) rolls the dice in the daily loser's game of who pays. This results in the much coveted annual Juan Valdez Loser's Award which includes a plaque and framed picture for the wall.

Anyone stopping by midmorning will catch the action as the 10 a.m. coffee club (a composition of businessmen of all distinctions) rolls the dice in the daily loser's game of who pays.

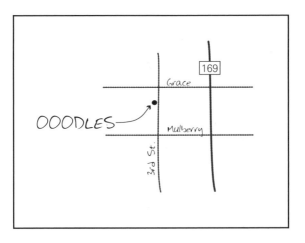

402 S. 3rd St., St. Peter, MN 56082
Hours: Mon - Thurs 4:30 a.m. - 8 p.m.
        Fri 4:30 a.m. - 9 p.m.
        Sat - Sun 4:30 a.m. - 2 p.m.
        Closed New Year's Day
Phone: 507-931-4455

SHERBURN

**CUP N' SAUCER
CATERING & CAFE**
21 N. Main
Sherburn, MN 56171

Cup n' Saucer

Since 1953 owner Pat Hanson has been creating wonderful pies and homemade meals. Recently honored as Martin County's senior citizen of the year, Pat at 72 still puts in her 10 -12 hour day at the Cup n' Saucer, while also creating meals-on-wheels and nutrition site community duties.

The restaurant, a short hop off I-90, is the city's favorite eating and greeting spot. Coffee and conversation come in abundant measure. The environment is vintage Americana.

Serving the best in homemade pies, creations include the traditional apple, peach and blueberry with specialties of coconut and raisin cream, similar to the Norsk Nook of Osseo, Wisconsin fame.

The favorite dishes of the often returning sales crowd are the Beef Commercial (bread, meat, mashed potatoes, gravy) and 10 oz. ribeye dinner. Lutefisk and lefse are offered in season.

Favorite dishes of the often returning sales crowd are the Beef Commercial and 10 oz. ribeye dinner.

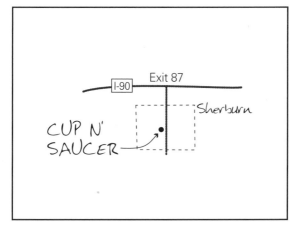

23 N. Main St., Sherburn, MN 56171

Hours: Mon - Tues, Thurs - Sat 7 a.m. - 8 p.m.
        Wed 7 a.m. - 2 p.m.
        Closed Sundays and Holidays

Smoking in designated area

Cash only

Phone: 507-764-6721

SHERBURN

Ma Faber's Home Cookin'

Sherburn, located on the I-90 corridor between Fairmont and Jackson, is the home of Ma Faber's.

The cafe's theme is birdhouses, with a warm use of ivy, family pictures and country curtains, creating a relaxed eating environment.

Diane (Ma) Faber spends approximately 90 hours a week in preparation of her home cooked meals, including homemade breads (also used for toast), rolls, salads and soups. Dinner specials include a Friday night fish fry and broasted chicken, all-you-can-eat combo, and a Saturday night prime rib.

This is a warm, sociable restaurant with a staff that takes special pride in personal attention to the customer.

Specials include Friday night fish fry and broasted chicken, all-you-can-eat combo, and Saturday night prime rib.

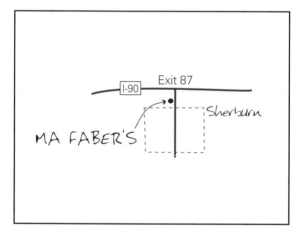

400 Hwy 4 N., Sherburn, MN 56171
Hours: Sun - Fri 6 a.m. - 8 p.m.
       Sat 6 a.m. - 9 p.m.
       Holidays 6 a.m. - 4 p.m.
Breakfast all day
Children's menu
Smoking in designated area
Credit cards: V, MC, D
Phone: 507-764-3116

SPICER

Annie's
Downtown Diner

Annie's Downtown Diner

Spicer, a relatively unknown touristy village on Lake Green, is the home of Annie's Downtown Diner. On Lake Avenue, the restaurant is adjacent to the lake frontage and city shops.

Customers complement the cafe for its fresh baked apple and rhubarb crisps. Breakfast, lunch and dinner selections are of the country cooking variety. The day begins with egg and pancake choices with real hash browns. Lunches offer a nice choice of salads. Dinners concentrate on the basics of chicken, beef and pork entrees along with fish and baskets.

The diner, spotlessly clean, has three separate dining rooms, each with a special theme. Decorations include plates, quilts, canisters and knick-knacks.

Antiques from Marilyn's attic and framed prints from local artist, Dorthea Paul, are available.

Customers complement the cafe for its fresh baked apple and rhubarb crisps.

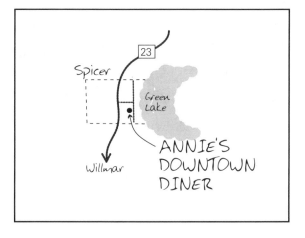

142 Lake Ave. N., Spicer, MN 56288

Hours: Mon - Fri 6 a.m. - 8 p.m.
Sat 6 a.m. - 8 p.m., Sun 6 a.m. - 1:30 p.m.
4th/July, Mon Holidays 6 a.m. - 1:30 p.m.
Closed Easter, Thanksgiving, Christmas

Breakfast served all day

Children's menu

Smoking in designated area

No credit cards

Phone: 320-769-5455

WILLMAR

TOWN TALK CAFE

Town Talk Cafe

The cafe may not be the site where the world's or even Minnesota's problems are solved, however, Town Talk, a 50-year-old institution, is favored by governors and politicians as the place to visit and learn from the people of west central Minnesota. As their logo implies, there is a lot of coffee consumed at the restaurant.

The cozy cafe, in downtown Willmar, has an environment featuring home decorating. The restaurant is located in the original Oddfellows building now, 104 years old.

The foods taste like coming home, and if Mom were there, she would agree. There is nothing better than simple foods well prepared. Begin the day with pancakes from Lorna Peterson's own buttermilk recipe or the special homemade apple rolls. Naturally, the large cinnamon and caramel rolls are also homemade. For egg eaters, the sausage and cheese omelette is a winner.

Lunches feature special "dinners" with choices that include hot dishes such as tator tot, hamburger and stroganoff entrees. Complementing the variety of specials are the usual lunchtime favorites. The choice between commercials beef and pork (bread, meat, mashed potatoes, gravy), burgers, melts, BLTs or homemade soup can be difficult.

Desserts favor two daily specials such as apple dumplings or cake and homemade cream and berry pies.

Begin with pancakes from Lorna Peterson's own buttermilk recipe of the special homemade apple rolls.

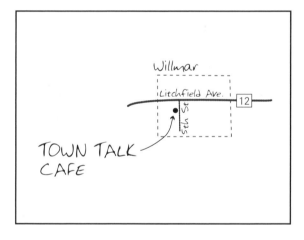

210 S.W. 5th St., Willmar, MN 56201

Hours: Mon - Fri 5 a.m. - 4 p.m.
         Sat 6 a.m. - 1 p.m.
         Closed Sundays and Holidays

Breakfast served all day

Children's menu

Smoking in designated area

Cash only

Phone: 320-235-0567

Southeast

ALBERT LEA

The Trumble's

Trumble's, a few short blocks from Exit 11 on I-35 toward Albert Lea, has been serving tourists and locals from this location for the last 14 years.

This spotless family restaurant offers an excellent variety of staple foods, all served by their friendly, efficient and professional staff, dressed in white and black.

On the sweet side, Trumble's provides jumbo muffins, cinnamon rolls, turtle cheesecake, fresh pies (including strawberry, in season), old fash-ioned root beer floats and tempting Tulip sundaes.

Breakfast entrees include traditional offerings and a distinctive hashbrown or taco omelette. Lunches are highlighted by an extensive sandwich menu, with choices of BBQ, pork tenderloin, roast pork and a variety of burgers. The dinner menu pro-vides variety touches of Polish franks and walleye.

For the weight conscious, there is a section devoted to the lighter appetite.

The dinner menu provides variety touches of Polish franks and walleye.

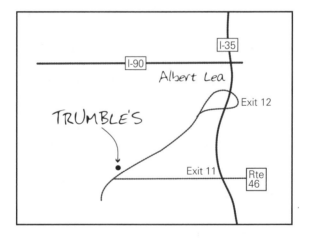

1811 E. Main St., Albert Lea, MN 56007
Hours: 6 a.m. - 10 p.m.
        Open daily except Christmas
Breakfast served all day
Children's menu (specially printed,
        includes puzzles and games)
Smoking in designated area
Credit cards: V, MC, D
Phone: 507-373-2638

ALDEN

MAIN STREET GRILL
ON BROADWAY

Main Street Grill

Alden, located at Exit 146 on I-90, is home to the Main Street Grill. The Danish heritage museum and city beach are both handy.

Open at 8 a.m. for coffee, rolls and conversation, the restaurant begins their lunch service at 10:30 a.m. The menu is small and simple concentrating on homemade preparations of the basics of beef, seafood, pork and chicken.

For lunch, sandwich entrees include pork tenderloin, fish, a BLT or burgers. Dinners involve a choice of steaks, beer battered seafood, breast of chicken and a center cut pork chop. Suppers are accompanied by a selection of potatoes and salads with homemade dressings. The Grill offers a winning selection of appetizers and a chef or taco salad for the lighter appetite. Thanks to an antique fountain service, a variety of malts, sundaes and cones are available.

The facilities are sparkling clean with a warm, casual atmosphere.

Known for great steaks and burgers, the Grill buys their products fresh each day from a local butcher.

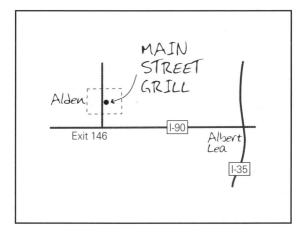

127 N. Broadway St., Alden, MN 56009
Hours: Mon - Sat 8 a.m. - 10 p.m.
          Closed Sun
Major credit cards accepted
Phone: 507-874-2648

ANNANDALE

Stanley's Family Restaurant

For well over 30 years, Stanley's has been preparing home-style meals for a cadre of loyal customers.

The menu is reasonably expansive. Daybreak starters include, for the seriously hungry, their Big Breakfast or Awesome Omelette (Nos. 10 and 13 respectively). For sandwiches at lunch, Stanley's offers a great open-faced steak with mushrooms, onions and Swiss cheese, or 20 plus other ideas not counting baskets, house favorites and salads.

Their home-style dinners are predictable and satisfying. Roast beef, meat loaf, liver and onions, pork chops, chicken and fish fill half a page, all served with a salad bar or soup plus a choice of seven potato side dishes.

The decor mirrors the town's theme of an 1800s western community and the nearby Minnesota Pioneer Park which includes several buildings of the pioneer era.

Daybreak starters include, for the seriously hungry, their Big Breakfast or Awesome Omelette.

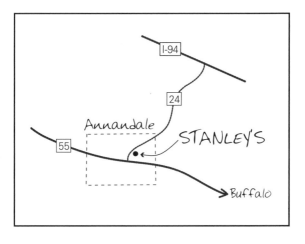

53 Oak Ave. N., Annandale, MN 55302

Hours: Mon - Thurs 6 a.m. - 9 p.m.
Fri - Sat 6 a.m. - 10 p.m.
Sun 7 a.m. - 8 p.m.
Open Holidays
(call for Holiday and Winter hours)

Children's menu

Smoking in designated area

Cash only

Phone: 320-274-8997

AUSTIN

The Old Mill Restaurant

The attraction for the Old Mill's ambiance is to dine as a welcomed guest. Featured in Midwest Living, their many returning patrons describe the environment as coming home again.

The dwelling for the restaurant is the original mill built in the late 1850s by two brothers from Lancshire, England. Converted to a restaurant in 1949, the old frame work and hand hewn beams and posts in the main dining room were preserved. Overlooking the Red Cedar River and Ramsey Dam, the Old Mill has become known as "the best little restaurant by a dam site."

Nutriments, served in the casual white linen atmosphere, feature seafood, steaks and owner-chef David Forland's special bone-in standing prime rib. Pastas and a lighter menu complement the main entrees.

Of historic interest, the dining area exhibits antiques from the family home of the mill's founders and decorative photos from the early milling days.

Featured in Midwest Living, their many returning patrons describe the environment as coming home again.

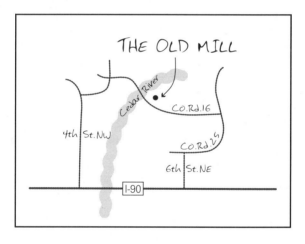

Rte. 1 Box 79A, Austin, MN 55912
Hours: Lunch: Mon - Fri 11:30 a.m. - 2 p.m.
        Dinner: Mon - Thurs 5:30 p.m. - 9 p.m.
            Fri - Sat 5:30 p.m. - 10 p.m.
        Closed Sundays
Smoking in designated area
Credit cards: V, MC, D, DN, CB
Phone: 507-437-2076

B

BELLE PLAINE

Tina-K's Cafe

Tina-K's, a very popular refuge for the hungry, is located on the west side of Highway 169 at Belle Plaine.

The cause for the lines of customers is their meals. Simply big and tasty. Breakfast begins with a four egg omelette, Belgian waffles and the Mountain Man entrée. Luncheon selections include croissant sandwiches and "Knife and Fork" burgers. Beef, ham and turkey commercials (bread, meat, mashed potatoes, gravy) are regular dinner favorites.

Homemade preparations include cream of asparagus soup, pies, cookies and donuts which are always available.

The Belle Plaine area is near to a number of destinations which offer shops, orchards and scenic drives.

Breakfast begins with a four egg omelette, Belgian waffles and the Mountain Man entrée.

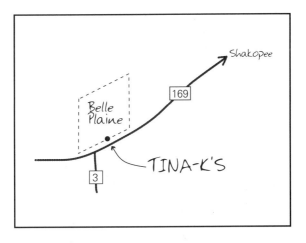

600 E. Poplar St., Belle Plaine, MN 56011
Hours: Mon - Sun 5 a.m. - 9 p.m.
     Winter: Mon 5 a.m. - 4:30 p.m.
        Tues - Sun 5 a.m. - 7:30 p.m.
     Open Holidays - call for hours
Breakfast anytime
Children's and seniors' menu
Smoking in designated area
Cash only
Phone: 952-873-2300

BELLE PLAINE

Emma Krumbees

Emma Krumbees is conveniently located on the east side of U.S. Highway 169 at Belle Plaine, a city midway between the Twin Cities and Mankato.

Described as a restaurant, bakery, deli, country store and orchard, the complex is a favorite stop for its loyal patrons. During October their renowned Annual Great Scarecrow Festival is held on the orchard grounds and has become a popular family tradition. Emma Krumbees offers quality food, superior service and a "whole lot of fun."

Pies with wonderfully flaky crusts are a specialty, many of which are fruit filled with homegrown ingredients. Pies-to-go are readily available. The restaurant serves a variety of dishes to accommodate everyone's appetite. Hearty beginnings include Emma's favorite and a country fried breaded pork tenderloin steak with hash browns and eggs. The Krumbee delux burger, Reuben, chicken pitas and a sourdough roast beef melt are among the luncheon choices. For dinner the entrees available include an "indescribable chow mein," Emma baked chicken and spaghetti and meatballs. A nice selection of salads complement the full menu.

Pies with wonderfully flaky crusts are a specialty, many of which are fruit filled with homegrown ingredients.

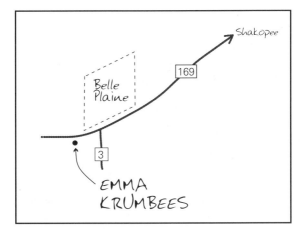

501 E. South St., Belle Plaine, MN 56011
Hours: 6 a.m. - 11 p.m., Daily
      Closed Christmas
Children's menu
Smoking in designated area
Credit cards accepted
Phone: 952-873-4334

C

CALEDONIA

Bluff Kountry Kafe

Located in Caledonia, the wild turkey capital of Minnesota, owner Shirley Pierce cares for her pleasant little cafe. Though prices alone are worth the drive, the great food is the real attraction.

The spic and span restaurant is as homey as any Granny's with edibles and service to match. Welcomed by the expression of "where good friends meet to eat," this is the perfect village choice for food and companionship.

For breakfast the Kingston Omelette is a must try. A reasonable selection of sandwiches, salads, baskets and the house special (a hot roast beef sandwich, the cafe's most popular choice) are available for midday dining.

Dinner selections include steaks, chicken, fish and meat loaf. All are served with a choice of potatoes, soup, salad or cole slaw and dinner roll. The all-you-can-eat, Friday fish fry is a regional favorite. Baked goods are all homemade.

Though prices alone are worth the drive, the great food is the real attraction.

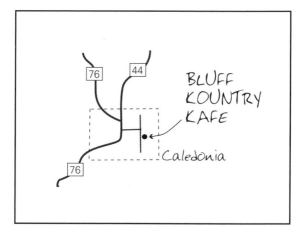

119 S. Kingston St., Caledonia, MN 55921

Hours: Mon - Thurs 5 a.m. - 6 p.m.
Fri 5 a.m. - 8 p.m.
Sat 5 a.m. - 5 p.m.
Sun 6 a.m. - 1 p.m.
Closed Christmas Day

Breakfast served all day

Smaller portions available

Smoking in designated area

Cash or check only

Phone: 507-724-5641

D

DASSEL

Red Rooster Cafe

The Red Rooster ("where breakfast is something to crow about") takes its name from Dassel's community theme. Originally the site of three chicken hatcheries, the town adopted the rooster as its mascot which is now used symbolically for the community's annual Labor Day and Red Rooster Days Festivals.

Eugene and Diana Skoog are the proud owners and operators of the little café which specializes in creating home-style meals. Breakfasts include Red Rooster Specials, bacon and eggs, pancakes, French toast and Country Breakfasts. Lunch offers daily specials, homemade soups and a dessert selection featuring an assortment of homemade pies and cakes.

Observing the communitiy's Norwegian heritage, the Red Rooster offers a lutefisk dinner daily beginning with the first full week in November through December 31. The diner's reputation attracts customers from many nearby (and some not so nearby) communities.

Observing the community's Norwegian heritage, the Red Rooster offers a lutefisk dinner daily beginning with the first full week in November through December 31.

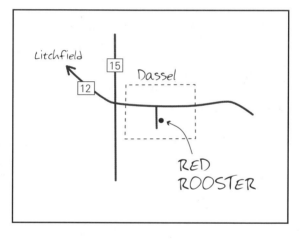

424-3rd St. N., (¹/₂ block so. of Hwy 12)
        Dassel, MN 55325
Hours: Mon - Fri 6 a.m. - 4 p.m.
        Sat 6 a.m. - 1 p.m., Sun 8 a.m. - 1 p.m.
Breakfast anytime
Smoking in designated area
Cash only
Phone: 320-275-3443

FARIBAULT

Bernie's Grill

Bernie's Grill has been voted as the best breakfast in Rice County with the menu anchored by biscuits and gravy and Blueberry cheese pancakes. There is some adventure in the luncheon menu as well with selections that range from shrimp scampi to chicken quesadillas.

The Elks building of 1918 construction is home to Bernie's with character supplied by a utilitarian atmosphere and fast, friendly service.

Bernie's Grill is in downtown Faribault adjacent to I-35. Named after fur trader, Alexander Faribault, the city offers tours of his 1853 home, and the River Bend Nature Center is located nearby.

Bernie's Grill has been voted as the best breakfast in Rice County.

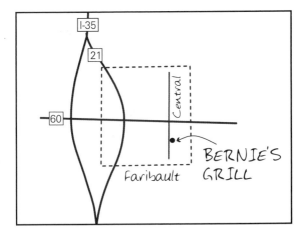

129 Central Ave. N., Faribault, MN 55021
Hours: 6 a.m. - 2 p.m.
          Closed Christmas, New Year's Day
Breakfast served all day
Children's menu
Smoking in designated area
Credit cards accepted
Phone: 507-334-7476

FARIBAULT

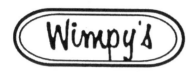

Wimpy's

Directions to Wimpy's are simple, "ask anyone in Faribault." This is a town focal point for coffee and socializing.

Mike Murphy, the cafe's owner since 1981, notes the restaurant has changed little since its beginning in 1936. This is a grand example of a traditional coffee shop.

Wimpy's offers honest food at very reasonable prices with a abundance of their free "news." The low-priced breakfast special of eggs, potatoes and toast is unbeatable. Choices from the large family menu will please most every appetite and includes daily specials and basic dinner entrees. Their fresh pies are made daily and generally in the oven early when the restaurant opens for the "regulars."

Mike Murphy, the cafe's owner since 1981, notes the restaurant has changed little since its beginning in 1936.

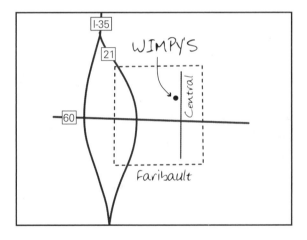

520 Central Ave. N., Faribault, MN 55021
Hours: Daily 5 a.m. - 9 p.m.
Phone: 507-334-4996

G

GLENCOE

Bump's Family Restaurant

Mike and Vicki Bump are proud of their newly remodeled family restaurant and its 11 years of service to the Glencoe community.

The environment is a bustling one - this is a busy place. A lot of goodwill is imparted by the friendly service and country foods. The Bumps describe their restaurant as a place where the coffee is always brewing and meals are made with a home-made taste. Lunches are the real thing including beef and turkey commercials (bread, meat, mashed potatoes, gravy) with scratch potatoes. Bump Burgers are a specialty using their own fresh ground beef. The pressure fried chicken is both a popular eat-in or take out choice.

The breakfast assortment includes French toast, waffles, eggs and a variety of homemade muffins and rolls.

Bump burgers are a specialty using their own fresh ground beef.

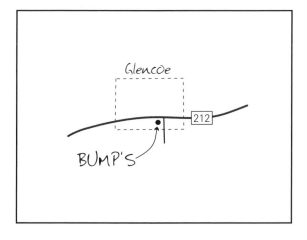

737 Morningside Dr., Glencoe, MN 55336
Hours: Mon - Sat 6 a.m. - 9 p.m.
         Sun 7 a.m. - 9 p.m.
         Closed Holidays
Breakfast served all day
Children's menu
Smoking in designated area
Credit cards: V, MC, D
Phone: 320-854-6038

HAMPTON

Little Oscar's Family Restaurant

Located in Hampton since 1964, Little Oscar's has been recognized by the *Minneapolis Star and Tribune* Taste Section for their quality of food and service.

With the unmistakable railroad theme, including a model train circling throughout the dining area, the restaurant provides a complete selection of meal time foods.

Breakfast meat of choice is often Little Oscar's signature bacon which is available with most daybreak dishes. Roundhouse Breakfast Meals include ham steak, the Engineer and Oscar's favorite. A sample of their lunch ideas are a Caboose Burger or a Big Oscar and a sandwich menu of grilled ham, melts, cod and chicken. Homemade soups are prepared daily with their great northern bean soup with ham always available. A complete selection of salads adds to the variety. Oven-baked chicken and grilled chicken breasts are dinner features.

Desserts include a Little Oscar's own homemade cinnamon roll, malts or shakes and especially their fresh pies. The award winning sour cream raisin and toasted coconut are customer favorites.

The award winning sour cream raisin and toasted coconut pies are customer favorites.

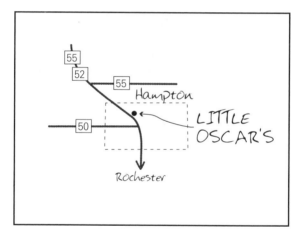

23470 Emery Ave., Hampton, MN 55031

Hours: Daily 6 a.m. - 9 p.m. Mem. Day - Labor Day
        Daily 6 a.m. - 8 p.m. Remainder of year
        Closed major Holidays

Breakfast served to 11a.m.- limited selections
        available to close

Children's menu

Smoking in designated area

Credit cards: V, MC, D, AE

Phone: 507-263-3322

HARMONY

THE
HARMONY HOUSE
RESTAURANT

The Harmony House Restaurant

Inaugurated as a restaurant in 1965, the Harmony House is situated in the heart of Minnesota's Amish community. This location makes the restaurant ideal for visiting and shopping with Amish wares sold both in the town and general area.

Reflecting the Amish tradition, The Harmony House is well known for its homemade foods. As owners Rodney and Marilyn Gregerson attest, these meals are like "grandma used to make."

House specialties include pies baked fresh daily in their own kitchen and homemade cinnamon, caramel and dinner rolls. Lunch specials are especially popular with a meat entrée, real mashed potatoes and gravy, vegetable, roll and salad. Evening and Sunday noon feature a homemade salad bar with rolls and lefse. Lite plate specials are also available.

Reflecting the Amish tradition,
The Harmony House is well known
for its homemade foods.

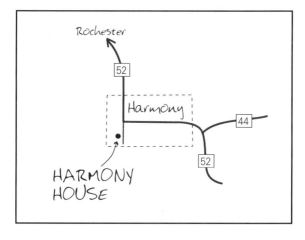

57 Main Ave. N., Harmony, MN 55939
Hours: Sun - Thurs 5 a.m. - 8 p.m.
        Fri - Sat 5 a.m. - 9 p.m.
        Closed Holidays
Breakfast served all day (no omelettes after 10:45)
Smoke free dining room
Smoking in designated area
No credit cards
Phone: 507-866-4612

HARTLAND

Village Inn

Village Inn

This vintage home-style café has been tended by owner Judy Hendrickson since 1985 As Judy relates, "it's the only hometown newspaper we have."

Neither the community nor the menu appear complex. This is pure home-style food honestly made to satisfy the basic appetite.

Breakfasts of eggs, meat and potatoes are the usual request with the homemade caramel roll a popular second. Lunches include a daily special in addition to the dinner and sandwich menu.

Dinners are accompanied by a choice of salads, vegetables and real mashed potatoes. Homemade soup is available everyday along with a sandwich menu. Judy does introduce seasonal dishes such as lefse and meat balls, and occasionally ethnic foods to her menu.

The Village Inn's pies are made fresh daily.

Breakfasts of eggs, meat and potatoes are the usual request with the home-made caramel roll a popular second.

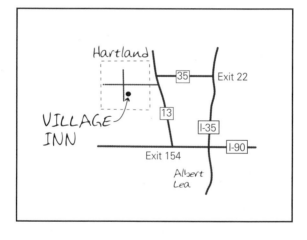

512 Broadway St., Hartland, MN 56042
Hours: Mon - Fri 6 a.m. - 4:30 p.m.
Sat 6 a.m. - 1 p.m.
Closed Sundays and Holidays
Smaller portions available
Smoking in designated area
Cash only
Phone: 507-845-2374

HOWARD LAKE

Red's Family Restaurant

It may be surprising to find that some of Minnesota's best pizza has a Howard Lake address. It just happens to be true.

Red's has been a café for the last 42 years. Since 1988 present owners, Bill and Gloria Strandquist, have been turning out scratch pizzas from the original Red's recipe. Their dough, tomato sauce, sausage and spaghetti sauce are all homemade. This popular fare has given the restaurant a customer base far beyond the city limits.

With charming service, the family restaurant also serves breakfast, lunch and dinner in the well worn, woody and congenial dining room.

Breakfast selections feature the usual and enjoyable range of starters such as eggs, 'cakes and a variety of meats.

Lunchtime favorites are the sub choices. Double hamburgers, Italian meatballs and French dip are among the selections, all served on a fresh 9" French roll available with or without fries. The café also has a pizza and 25 item salad buffet from 11 a.m. - 2. p.m.

Dinners include a variety of tempting choices from a ribeye steak to chicken specialties. Red's well-known Friday fish fry features fresh fish breaded in their own kitchen.

The all-you-can-eat Sunday brunch (10 a.m. - 2 p.m.) features a variety of homemade foods.

It may be surprising to find that some of Minnesota's best pizza has a Howard Lake address.

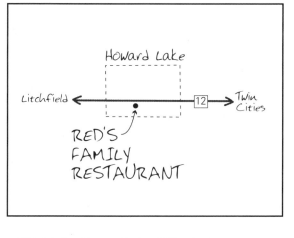

728-6th St., Howard Lake, MN 55349

Hours: Mon - Thurs 8 a.m. - 11 p.m.
          Fri 8 a.m. - 2 a.m.
          Sat 7:30 a.m. - 2 a.m.
          Sun 10 a.m. - 10 p.m.
          Closed Easter, Thanksgiving and Christmas

Kids corner menu

Smoking in designated area

Credit cards: V, MC, D, AE

Phone: 320-543-3331

JORDAN

Feed Mill Restaurant

The old fashioned red shingled building, which the Feed Mill now calls home, had been a working feed mill in the Jordan community.

The Jordan River, visible through the cafe's bank of windows, contributes to the restaurant's charm as does the small antique store adjacent to the restaurant. The cafe also hosts the owners' coin collection with hundreds of coins on display and for purchase.

The menu offers some innovations from the norm; breakfast of wild rice pancakes, a bacon-egg and melted cheese on toast sandwich or an extra-large ham and cheese omelette. For lunch a sirloin burger or their Farmers Special on homemade bread are popular selections. The dinner combinations of barbeque ribs and chicken, and the chicken and ham entrees are enjoyable combinations.

The Sunday brunch begins at 8:30 a.m., attracting a number of repeat and regular customers.

The Jordan River, visible through the cafe's bank of windows, contributes to the restaurant's charm.

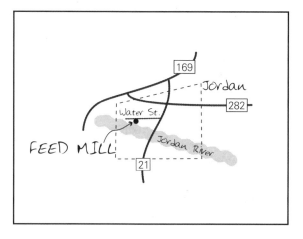

200 Water St. Jordan, MN 55352-1519

Hours: Tues - Thurs 7 a.m. - 3 p.m.
　　　 Fri - Sat 7 a.m. - 7 p.m.
　　　 Sun 8:30 a.m. - 2 p.m.
　　　 Closed Mondays

Children's menu

Smoking in designated area

Credit cards: V, MC, AE

Phone: 952-492-3646, 800-723-8499

KASSON

Daniel's Restaurant

Over one hundred thousand customers a year is the measure Daniel's uses to define popular. The foods – delightful, delicious and as home-style as ever prepared account for their packed house.

Since 1977, Dan and Marg Gadient have committed themselves to providing high quality meals and service. Their three daughters also work in the family business. Dan is in the kitchen most days creating entrees like their popular boneless pork chop dinner or sandwiches served on their homemade bread. The sensational Friday night, all-you-can-eat batter dipped cod special may require a short wait – it's that good.

Mornings start with homemade cinnamon and caramel rolls – a meal in themselves; naturally, all the comfortable breakfast choices are available.

Desserts are a specialty. Cheesecake, double raspberry, turtle and earthquake, are irresistible, as is the deep (3½") dish Kentucky Bourbon pecan pie. All are made-from-scratch.

Sensational Friday night, all-you-can-eat batter dipped cod special, may require a wait – it's that good.

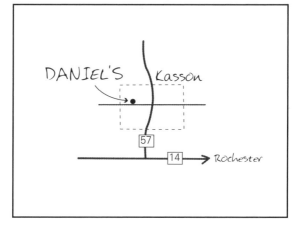

19 W. Main St., Kasson, MN 55944-1454

Hours: Mon - Thurs 5:30 a.m. - 9 p.m.
        Fri 5:30 a.m. -10 p.m.
        Sat 5:30 a.m. - 9 p.m.
        Sun 6:30 a.m. - 9 p.m.
        Closed Thanksgiving and Christmas

Breakfast served all day

Children's menu

Smoking in designated area

Credit cards accepted

Phone: 507-634-7775

KELLOGG

Town and Country Cafe

Town and Country Cafe

The Town and Country, with easy access to Highway 61, is a family style restaurant with a homemade menu. This cafe offers hearty breakfasts, luncheon specials, and fresh pies and desserts including cakes and cobblers.

Home of Lark Toys, a unique specialty toy shop, Kellogg offers craft and antique shopping.

As this section of the state is a popular hunting area, the cafe uses a decor of mounted animals including deer, turkey, bear and muskie.

The mother and daughter owners, Thelma and Patti Holland, have been creating their quality foods for the last ten years.

This cafe offers hearty breakfasts, luncheon specials, and fresh pies and desserts including cakes and cobblers.

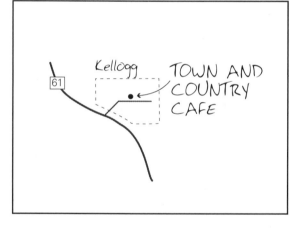

309 E. Belvidere Ave. Kellogg, MN 55945

Hours: Mon - Wed 6 a.m. - 4 p.m.
         Thurs 6 a.m. - 8 p.m., Fri 6 a.m. - 9 p.m.
         Sat 6 a.m. - 8 p.m., Sun 6:30 a.m. - 1 p.m.

Children's menu

Smoking in designated area

No credit cards

Phone: 507-767-4593

LAKE CITY

Chickadee Cottage
Tea Room & Restaurant

Since the perfect setting for a Tea Room and Restaurant named the Chickadee Cottage would be a 100 year old restored home, this is exactly where the visitor will find Lake City's charming eatery.

Serving breakfast, lunch and afternoon tea (2:30 p.m. - 4:30 p.m.) in either the Wedding Room, porch or gazebo, surrounded by perennials and herb gardens, diners enjoy the finest in from-scratch cooking including soups, breads and desserts.

The menus offer some wonderful choices making decisions somewhat difficult. Special scrambled eggs, French toast prepared with fine-textured Italian bread, polenta or biscuits and gravy are everyday breakfast entrees as are daily specials at attractive prices. On Saturdays the "Cottage" adds caramel rolls, Swedish pancakes, eggs Benedict and Morning-style eggs, with Sunday featuring their Family Style Breakfast which has a highly regarded regional reputation – expect a crowd.

Adventuresome lunches begin with wonderful appetizers of Pear and Blue Cheese Crepes, Polenta with Pesto and Tomato or a Mediteranean Plate. Main courses include sandwiches (Wild Rice Burger, Dutch Treat, Chicken Pita), salads, soup or scones. For a unique luncheon experience the restaurant prepares a Tea Plate, Tea Lunch or Londonerry Tea.

Adventuresome lunches begin with wonderful appetizers of Pear and Blue Cheese Crepes, Polenta with Pesto and Tomato or a Mediteranean Plate.

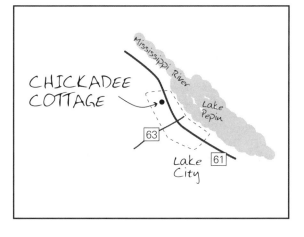

317 N. Lakeshore Dr., Lake City, MN 55041
Hours: Tues - Sat 7:30 a.m. - 4:30 p.m.
       (Breakfast to 11 a.m.)
       Sun 8 a.m. - 4:30 p.m.
       (Sun Family Breakfast to 2 p.m.)
Children's menu
No smoking
Credit cards accepted
Phone: 651-345-5155, 888-321-5177

LAKE CITY

The Galley

Sports minded Lake City is located on highway 61 as it parallels the Mississippi between Red Wing and Wabasha.

As a boating and tourist area, the city hosts both summer and winter festivals including its June celebration as the birthplace of water skiing, Appleseed Days in October and Winterfest in February.

Featuring a Friday night fish fry and Sunday breakfast buffet, the Galley offers family dining with a wide variety of menu items. Breakfast, lunch and dinner specials are offered daily. The café is noted for the best breakfast in town.

In keeping with its name and setting, the Galley has a nautical theme. Nautical items are also for sale in the Nautical Nook area of the restaurant.

The café is noted for the best breakfast in town.

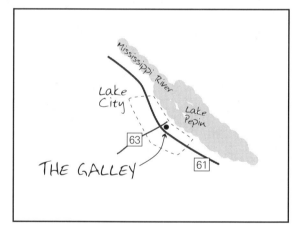

100 E. Lyon Ave. (Intersection Hwys 61 a n d 63)
    Lake City, MN 55041
Hours: 6 a.m. - 8 p.m. Daily
    Winter hours may vary
Breakfast served to 11 a.m. Mon - Fri
    11:30 a.m. Sat - Sun
Children's menu
Credit cards: V, MC, D
Phone: 651-345-9991

L

LANESBORO

Trail Inn Cafe

With an address in the middle of Lanesboro's mix of absorbing shops, from a meat market to antiques, the Trail Inn is a perfect rendezvous.

Visitors to the area enjoy cycling the Root River Bike Trail or canoeing the river itself. Nearby, the state parks of Forestville and Beaver Creek Valley have wonderful hiking trails.

Satisfying the appetite of the scores of tourists, the Trail Inn provides a wide assortment of choices.

The lunch crowd can choose between an extensive list of appetizers, homemade pizza (from scratch) or 21 different sandwiches. Dinner choices expand the entrees to include famous broasted chicken and steaks. Daily homemade specials include ice cream treats and fresh pie.

The lunch crowd can choose between an extensive list of appetizers, homemade pizza (from scratch) or 21 different sandwiches.

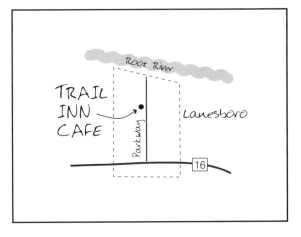

111 Parkway Ave., Lanesboro, MN 55949

Hours: Memorial Day - Labor Day
          Mon - Sat 11 a.m. - 8 p.m.,
          Sun 11 a.m. - 7 p.m.
      Labor Day - Memorial Day
          Tues - Sat 11 a.m. - 8 p.m.
          Sun 11 a.m. - 7 p.m.
      Closed Mondays

Children's menu

Smoking in designated areas

Cash only

Phone: 507-467-2200

MANTORVILLE

The Hubbell House

One of Minnesota's oldest operating dining establishments, The Hubbell House, offers a rare opportunity to step back to the Civil War era and enjoy a memorable dining experience.

Housed in a National Historic site, constructed in 1856, the restaurant's authenticity is evident in the attention to detail. Antiques, historic documents, paneled dining rooms with wallpaper dating to the 1800s era and fixtures devoted to memorabilia, vintage china and civil war mementos create a dining adventure.

Since 1946, the Pappas family has carried forward the highest standards in food preparation and has been recognized for its quality by the receipt of numerous awards.

The presentation is on placemats accompanied by fine table settings including custom made china and crystal. Placemats used by the Hubbell House are famous for bearing the signature of distinguished guests from the 1800s and 1900s. The menu features American dishes with choices which include steaks, Minnesota walleye, chicken, ribs and vegetarian dishes.

The village of Mantorville also provides the visitor an opportunity to browse through specialty shops and experience buildings of historic interest.

Housed in a National Historic site, constructed in 1856, the restaurant's authenticity is evident in the attention to detail.

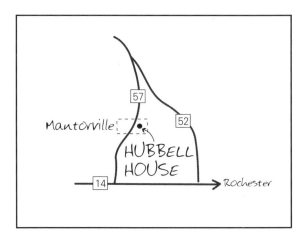

Hwy 57, Mantorville, MN 55955
Hours: Tues - Sat 11:30 a.m. - 2 p.m.
            5 p.m. to close
            Sun 11:30 a.m. to close
            Closed Mon
Reservations suggested
Children's menu
No smoking
All credit cards accepted
Phone: 507-635-2331, fax: 507-635-5280

NEW PRAGUE

Schumacher's New Prague Hotel and Restaurant

Entering the New Prague Hotel, the visitor accepts the invitation to "Step into the warmth and charm of a European Inn."

The historic hotel was established in 1898 as the Broz Hotel with renovation by owner, John Schumacher, beginning in 1974. With 16 distinctive guest rooms, the hotel is now a Minnesota Institution.

Our primary interest is the authenticity of the kitchen which creates exceptional meals for breakfast, lunch and dinner patrons.

John, an internationally known executive chef, prepares Central European cuisine of German and Czechoslovakian origin including wiener schnitzel, roast duck, Czech sausage and the irresistible kolaches. Game dishes such as elk are prepared to order. Kathleen Schumacher is responsible for both the healthy heart section of the menu and the outstanding selection of items in the European Gift shop.

The ambiance includes the Old World charm of Bavarian chandeliers.

John, an internationally known executive chef, prepares Central European cuisine of German and Czechoslovakian origin.

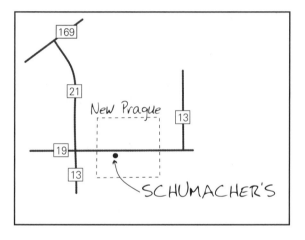

212 W. Main St., New Prague, MN 56071
Hours: 11:30 a.m. - 9 p.m. Daily
Breakfast served to overnight guests only
Children's menu
Smoking permitted in bar area only
Credit cards accepted
Phone: 952-758-2133

NEW RICHLAND

Sweets Ltd.

Sweets is located in the small farming community of New Richland. The restaurant has the feel of informality found only in the unhurried pace of a cafe where everyone is just simply friendly and the food down-home.

For the last 12 years Linda Timmerman and Barb Thompson have operated their neat and tidy restaurant to the delight of their loyal customers.

The visitor can look forward to "good old home cooking," as Linda and Barb describe the menu. Breakfasts include the staples of eggs, meat and potatoes with pancakes, waffles and French toast available. Lunch is a busy time for the cafe with homemade soup and a nice assortment of sand-wiches and burgers keeping the kitchen active. Specials are always on the menu with their home-made pies a popular choice.

The atmosphere is comfortable with the wall deco-rated by historic pictures of the New Richland community.

Specials are always on the menu with their homemade pies a popular choice.

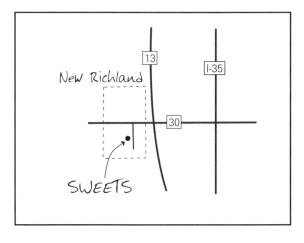

224-2nd St. S.E., New Richland, MN 56072
Hours: Mon - Fri 6 a.m. - 4 p.m.
　　　　Sat 7 a.m. - 1 p.m.
　　　　Closed Sun and Holidays
Smoking in designated area
No credit cards
Phone: 507-465-8014

NORTHFIELD

Ole Store Cafe

Ole Store Cafe

(Home of the Famous Ole Roll)

In terms of special places, they don't come any nicer than the Ole Store.

Excellent service, wonderful ambience and a great selection of edibles are the reasons to take advantage of this Northfield vintage cafe.

Special selections to start the day include Eggs Lorraine, a seafood omelette or the ham and cheddar scramble. These go nicely with their own recipe breakfast sausage or made-from-scratch waffles and pancakes. In the area, a weekend must is the Cafe's Saturday and Sunday brunch which features all the weekday breakfast specials. Naturally, the famous Ole Roll is always a tempting choice.

Briefly noting the luncheon menu, homemade creations begin with soups, especially the very popular chicken and wild rice creation. The sandwich board includes chicken salad, a wonderful grilled Reuben and a grilled Swiss, ham and tomato. Satisfying the dinner appetite, the Ole Store prepares a basil-raspberry chicken breast, a pork loin marsala, pan-fried walleye or a seafood pasta.

The ambiance is equally exciting. Home is a building with heritage beginning in 1889 and set on a tree-lined residential street one block from the St. Olaf campus.

The turn of the century atmosphere is apparent from the curbside architecture and the interior of wooden floors, high ceilings and authentic Rosemalen antiques.

Home of the Famous Ole Roll.
In terms of special places, they don't
come any nicer than the Ole Store.

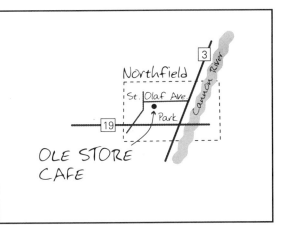

1011 St. Olaf Ave., Northfield, MN 55057

Hours: Tues - Fri 6:30 a.m. - 2 p.m.
        Sat - Sun 7:30 a.m. - 2 p.m.
        Fri and Sat evenings 5 p.m. - 8:30 p.m.
        Closed Mon

No smoking

Major credit cards accepted

Phone: 507-645-5558

NORTHFIELD

TREATS, LTD.

Treats, Ltd.

With this distinctive restaurant, the customer has a choice between formal dining or their busy, casual, upscale deli. The restaurant's location is ideal for visitors to the downtown historic area with buildings dating to the 1800s.

The menu is invigorating, with choices which include a wide variety of ethnic foods changing by day and season. Daily entrees include diverse offerings such as leek pie, moussaka, pasta, cornish pasties or a shepherds pie.

Seasonally from Labor Day to Memorial Day authentic Indian curries are available.

Breakfast on Saturday and Sunday includes specialty pancakes, omelettes and eggs Benedict.

A wide range of gourmet items are available for purchase.

Daily entrees include diverse offerings such as leek pie, moussaka, pasta, cornish pasties or a shepherds pie.

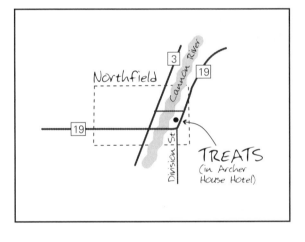

214 Division St. S., (Archer House Hotel)
    Northfield, MN 55057
Hours: Mon - Fri 7 a.m. - 8 p.m.
        Sat - Sun 8 a.m. - 5 p.m.
Beer and Wine available
No smoking
Major credit cards accepted
Phone: 507-663-0050

OWATONNA

Costas' Candies and Restaurant

Costas' is located on Cedar Avenue adjacent to Owatonna's city square. This marvelous little cafe has been a family tradition since 1920. In 1960, owner Costas Boosalis purchased the restaurant from his uncle who taught him the art of creating his original homemade candies.

The menu is Greek-oriented, offering specialties such as a feta or gyro omelette for breakfast or their famous Greek salad for lunch or dinner. Desserts include baklava or kourambiedies (butter cookies).

Their candy selections include English toffee, butter caramels, nut clusters, or popular cremes, all made from family recipes. Costas' receives country wide requests for these wonderful sweets unequaled in quality and taste.

Costas' receives country wide requests for these wonderful sweets unequaled in quality and taste.

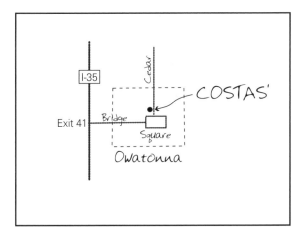

112 N. Cedar, Owatonna, MN 55060

Hours: Mon - Fri 7:30 a.m. - 6:30 p.m.
Sat 7:30 a.m. - 4:30 p.m.
Closed Sun and Holidays

Breakfast served to 11 a.m.

Smoking in designated area

No credit cards

Phone: 507-451-9050

OWATONNA

The Kitchen

The Kitchen, a popular local cafe with many customers on a first name basis, has been in downtown Owatonna since 1962.

The food is staple and abundant featuring real home cooked meals. The bill of fare has some nice choices. Corned beef hash, a build-your-own omelette (all omelettes are prepared with three eggs) and a large ála carte section all very reasonably priced. Their specialty sandwich selections include BBQ pork, turkey melt, a double decker, stacked beef and a hot ham. Soup of the day is homemade and homemade chili is available in season. Beef, seafood, pork and chicken entrees are on the dinner listing.

The Owatonna community has a number of attractions, among them, the Arts Center and the interesting State Orphanage Museum.

Specialty sandwich selections include BBQ pork, turkey melt, a double decker, stacked beef and a hot ham.

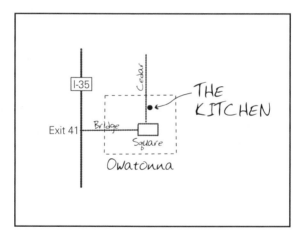

329 N. Cedar Ave., Owatonna, MN 55060
Hours: Mon - Sat 6 a.m. - 9 p.m.
           Closed Sun and Holidays
Breakfast served all day
Children's menu
Smoking in designated area
No credit cards
Phone: 507-451-9991

PINE ISLAND

Whispering Pines Family Restaurant

Pine Island's Main Street is home to the Whispering Pines Family Restaurant located in the towns former Opera House constructed in the 1800s.

This busy restaurant, operated by Nathan and Heather Tiarks, has recently been remodeled and offers a complete menu with daily lunch and dinner specials. Their Friday night walleye special is a popular event served in the cozy pine atmosphere. A salad bar is available after 5 p.m.

In addition to being located near the popular Douglas Trail bike bath, they offer both framed art work and crafts for sale.

Their Friday night walleye special is a popular event served in the cozy pine atmosphere.

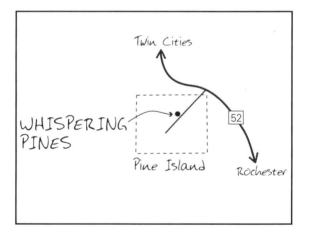

212 S. Main St., Pine Island, MN 55963
Hours: Mon - Sat 6 a.m. - 8 p.m.
        Closed Sundays
Breakfast served all day
Kids corner menu
Senior citizen discounts
Smoking in designated area
No credit cards
Phone: 507-356-2455

R

RED WING

Braschler's
Bakery & coffee SHOP

Braschler's Bakery & Coffee Shop

The Bakery and Coffee Shop is conveniently located in the heart of Red Wing. The cafe prepares hearty home-style sandwiches, chili and soups. An unlimited fresh salad bar is offered Monday through Friday. Coffee, fresh pastries and deli items are offered in a homey and customer friendly environment.

Bob and Nancy purchased the Bakery in 1972 with the stipulation by the previous owners that they continue making the unique Swedish Limpa Rye Bread. This special bread is available fresh every Friday and Saturday.

The quality of their baked goods is evidenced by its presence in many of Red Wing's finer restaurants.

Their unique Swedish Limpa Rye Bread is available fresh every Friday and Saturday.

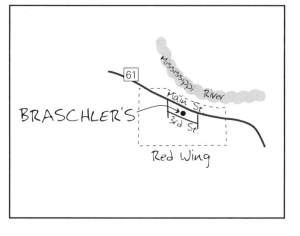

410 W. 3rd St., Red Wing, MN 55066
Hours: Bakery: Mon - Fri 6 a.m. - 5 p.m.
        Sat 6 a.m. - 3 p.m.
      Coffee Shop: Mon - Fri 7 a.m. - 4 p.m.
        Sat 7 a.m. - 3 p.m.
      Closed Sun and Holidays
No smoking
Credit cards: V, MC, D, AE
Phone: 651-388-1580

ROCHESTER

Cheap Charlie's Cafe

As a traditional hash house, there are few comparable to Cheap Charlie's. Began in 1955 and now owned by David Tran, the cafe's authenticity can be traced to the wellworn, emblematic pig sitting atop the roof.

The crowd at Charlies doesn't linger over their meal. This bustling cafe serves foods in abundance and quickly. Most customers of this Rochester landmark arrive from the industrial and warehouse surroundings.

Their filling meals are not fancy. Big ham and egg platters, beef or pork dinners with real mashed potatoes and daily specials are the meals of choice. The atmosphere is the result of people in motion and the cafe's appealing camaraderie.

Big ham and egg platters, beef or pork dinners with real mashed potatoes and daily specials are the meals of choice.

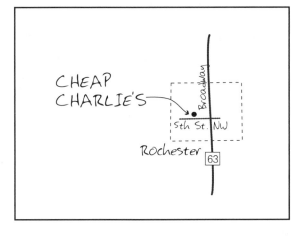

11-5th St. N.W., Rochester, MN 55901

Hours: Mon - Fri 5 a.m. - 7 p.m.
         Sat 5 a.m. - 1 p.m.
         Closed Sun and Holidays

Breakfast served all day

Smoking in designated area

Cash or check only

Phone: 507-289-7693

ROCHESTER

Grandma's Kitchen

Though a bit ordinary in appearance due to its location in a modest mall, Grandma's Kitchen is a true blue American cafe.

As its boisterous, crowded clientele attest, this is where Rochester finds real farm cooking.

The patrons breakfast on basic egg and meat dishes accompanied by real, fresh hash browns. The French toast and daily breakfast specials are local favorites.

Lunch is not so much a burger place, as the homemade hot beef and pork sandwiches with scratch gravy are more common selections.

Daily specials include roast turkey and dressing, Swiss steak or liver and onions. The homemade soups are always on the menu. For dessert, of course, there is pie. These are homemade and their special cream pies are made-from-scratch.

With the ambiance created by some antiques, the folksy country setting is the perfect place to enjoy high quality country cooking.

As its boisterous, crowded clientele attest, this is where Rochester finds real farm cooking.

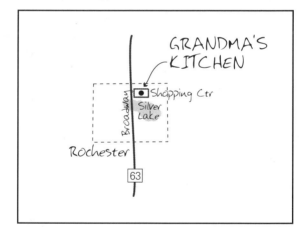

1514 N. Broadway, Rochester, MN 55906
        (Silver Lake Shopping Center)
Hours: Mon - Sat 6 a.m. - 8 p.m.
        Closed Sun and Holidays
Breakfast to 11 a.m.
Children menu
Smoking in designated area
Cash or check
Phone: 507-289-0331

RUSHFORD

MILL STREET
⇒ INN ⇐

Mill Street Inn

Early settlers in the area called Rushford the Trail City, and it remains a popular stopover or starting point for enthusiasts of the Root River State Trail.

Historically, the Mill Street Inn occupies a building constructed in 1870. Their 18" walls are from locally quarried limestone with a wood floor of original maple. Light fixtures are over 100 years old having been acquired from the remodeling of the Rushford School.

The Mill Street Inn features a famous Friday night fish fry, and offers a Saturday night prime rib. Pasta specialties include a ravioli, mostocioli, veal parmigiana and a wonderful toasted French bread. Homemade pies are a specialty.

Very reasonably priced breakfasts include the usual egg, meat, potato and 'cake variations. For lunch the cafe provides a full selection of burgers, soups and salads and sandwich specials.

Pasta specialties include a ravioli, mostocioli, veal parmigiana and a wonderful toasted French bread.

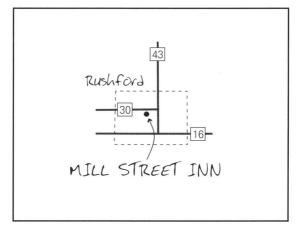

102 W. Jessie St. (corner Hwy 30 and Hwy 43)
       Rushford, MN 55971

Hours: Mon 6 a.m. - 2 p.m.
        Tues - Wed - Thurs 6 a.m. - 8 p.m.
        Fri - Sat 6 a.m. - 10 p.m.
        Sun 8 a.m. - 8 p.m.

Breakfast served until 10:30 a.m. weekdays,
        11 a.m. weekends

Smoking in designated area

No credit cards

Phone: 507-864-2929

ST. CHARLES

Del's Cafe

A hop off the Interstate, Del's Cafe is located on St. Charle's Main Street.

To the north of St. Charles is the popular Whitewater State Park noted for its natural beauty, trout streams and bluffland trails.

The cafe has been in the same location for over 40 years serving home-style cooking to the community with reasonably priced wholesome foods.

Breakfast selections include omelettes, biscuits and gravy, muffins and fresh cinnamon and caramel rolls. Specialty sandwiches, such as a western steak sandwich or a sliced prime rib melt highlight the noon menu. The dinner menu offers pork roast and dressing on Thursdays and a Friday favorite, all-you-can-eat fish and shrimp combination.

Specialty sandwiches, such as a western steak sandwich or a sliced prime rib melt, highlight the noon menu.

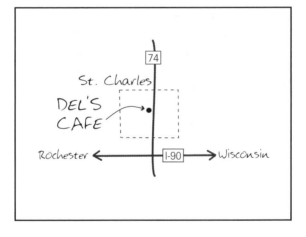

1012 Whitewater Ave., St. Charles, MN 55972
Hours: Sun - Thurs 5 a.m. - 9 p.m.
        Fri - Sat 5 a.m. - 10 p.m.
Breakfast anytime
Children's menu
Smoking in designated area
Cash only
Phone: 507-932-4514

S

SOUTH HAVEN

MOM'S PLACE

Mom's Place

Mom's Place is located on Highway 55 as it wanders through the Minnesota countryside west of Buffalo.

Mary Ann (Mom) and Steve (Pop) take turns preparing their homemade foods. Many dishes are created with recipes Mary Ann's mother used preparing dishes in her own kitchen. Even their sauces, BBQ, cheese and tarter, are homemade.

The cafe is a community center where locals come to chat and chew. Visitors receive special attention and a warm welcome from the friendly staff.

With hearty breakfasts, ⅓ pound burgers made from fresh beef, broasted chicken and homemade soups and salads, Mom's Place will satisfy the traveler's appetite.

Even their sauces – BBQ, cheese and tarter are homemade.

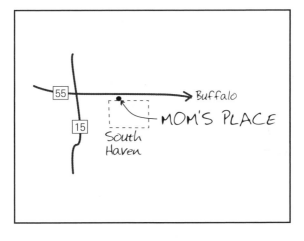

500 Custer St., South Haven, MN 55382

Hours: Summer: Mon - Sat 5 a.m. - 9 p.m.
           Sun 6 a.m. - 9 p.m.
        Winter: Mon - Thurs 6 a.m. - 8 p.m.
           Fri 6 a.m. - 9 p.m.
           Sat - Sun 6 a.m. - 9 p.m.
       Holidays 6 a.m. - 9 p.m.

Breakfast served all day

Children's menu

Smoking in designated area

Phone: 320-326-7559

SPRING GROVE

The Bake Shoppe

The site of The Bake Shoppe can be historically traced to 1880. Through a succession of interesting ownerships, the location has experienced several different businesses. Its reopening in 1988 as a restaurant was the result of community interest and request.

The present owner, Paola Utecht, varies the menu seasonally. For summer, in addition to the fresh bakery items, the features include deli sandwiches and homemade pies. Winter fare includes homemade soups and a variety of hot foods such as creamed chicken or turkey over baking powder biscuits.

The environment is a country setting including a pictorial history of the area. There are some crafts for sale.

For summer, in addition to the fresh bakery items, the features include deli sandwiches and homemade pies.

131 W. Main St., Spring Grove, MN 55974
(Southside, State Hwy 44)

Hours: Mon - Sat 7 a.m. - 4 p.m.
Sun 7 a.m. - 2 p.m.
Closed Holidays

Smoking in designated area

Cash only

Phone: 507-498-5482

SPRING VALLEY

Charlie's On Broadway

Charlie's On Broadway

Since license plates from Wisconsin, Iowa and Minnesota are apparent on Broadway in Spring Valley, it must be midday on Tuesday. That's when Charlie's serves up the famous Chicken and Biscuits.

This is the sort of restaurant where you would take Grandma – it's down-home comfortable and offers genuine, full-flavored foods, all served in a pleasant setting.

Everything is homemade beginning with their breakfast menu including a full Saturday breakfast special of eggs, meat, hash browns and toast at an unbeatable price.

Lunch includes a large salad bar, with homemade salads, ⅓ pound or bigger fresh burgers and daily specials. There is a small gift shop on the premises.

Spring Valley is located on Highway 63, a major north-south route in southern Minnesota.

This is the sort of restaurant where you would take Grandma – it's down-home comfortable.

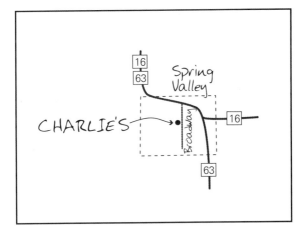

136 N. Broadway, Spring Valley, MN 55975
Hours: Mon - Sat 5:30 a.m. - 4 p.m.
        Closed Sun and Holidays
Breakfast served to 11 a.m.
Children's menu and senior discounts
Cash only
Phone: 507-346-9848

WABASHA

The Anderson House
WABASHA, MINNESOTA 55981

The Anderson House

The Anderson House is Minnesota's oldest operating Country Inn, having been run by the same family for 142 years. The Inn, located one block from the Mississippi River, is furnished in antiques, most dating back to 1856, and truly represents the finest in historic atmosphere and decor. Shuttles are available to and from the local marinas.

The restaurant features a complete menu from Grandma Anderson's Famous Dutch Kitchen where all food is made-from-scratch with homemade cookies, breads and pies baked daily. The Giant Dutch Cinnamon Rolls are a special and unique treat.

As a testament to its quality, the Anderson House has been featured nationally in such venues as the CBS evening news, *People Magazine*, *Ladies Home Journal* and the *Wall Street Journal*.

The restaurant features a complete menu from Grandma Anderson's Famous Dutch Kitchen where all food is made-from-scratch.

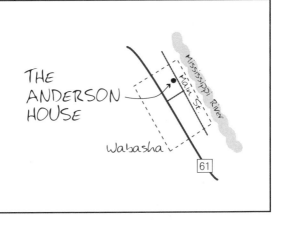

333 W. Main St., Wabasha, MN 55981

Hours: May to December 1
                Mon - Fri 8 a.m. - 9 p.m.
                Sat - Sun 7 a.m. - 9 p.m.
                Sunday Brunch 8:30 a.m. - 1 p.m.

         December 1 to March
            Full service weekends
            Limited service weekdays

No smoking

Credit cards accepted

Phone: 651-565-4524, 800-535-5467

WASECA

Busy Bee Cafe

The cafe's name well describes this hometown restaurant established on Waseca's main north-south street. There has been a Busy Bee restaurant for over 40 years.

There is comfort in the vintage menu of home-made foods. Selections are traditional and include a complete list of hot and cold sandwiches, fresh made salads and homemade soups. Dinners of a hamburger steak commercial (bread, meat, mashed potatoes, gravy), ham steak, and special-ty dinners of fish, shrimp and chicken strips are prepared daily.

Pies, cakes and cookies are all homemade and are served with a dessert menu of sundaes, root beer floats, shakes and malts.

Morning starters from the kitchen consist of cus-tomary egg favorites, biscuits and gravy and French toast made with cinnamon bread.

The squeaky clean cafe uses antique cooking items to create charm and character.

Pies, cakes and cookies are all homemade and are served with a dessert menu of sundaes, root beer floats, shakes and malts.

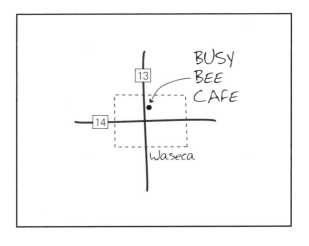

214 N. State St., Waseca, MN 56093

Hours: Mon - Fri 5:30 a.m. - 4 p.m.
        Sat 5:30 a.m. - 1:30 p.m.
        Closed Sun and Holidays

Breakfast served until 11 a.m.

Smoking in designated area

Credit cards accepted

Phone: 507-835-9908

WATERVILLE

The Waterville Cafe

To stop by the Waterville Cafe for some really great food is also to visit one of Minnesota's more unique cafes. As the owners' hobby is classic bicycles, they happen to be everywhere, including suspended from the ceiling. By chance, this identifies with the city's location on the 39-mile Sakatah Singing Hills Bike Trail.

The cafe has a large menu – for example, 11 omelette choices and a complete selection of lunch and dinner items. Meatball sub, meat loaf commercial (bread, meat, mashed potatoes, gravy), sausage options and their slow roasted prime rib, available any time, are all customer preferences.

Fresh salads (eight choices) and homemade soups cover the basics, with a hot lunch buffet featured Monday-Friday from 11 a.m. to 2 p.m. The Friday fish fry is an all-you-can-eat, batter-dipped cod. Sunday brunch is from 10 a.m. to 2 p.m.

The wonderful food is all prepared by owners Pat and Shannon Clark who both received their training from the New England Culinary Institute.

The wonderful food is all prepared by owners Pat and Shannon Clark who both received their training from the New England Culinary Institute.

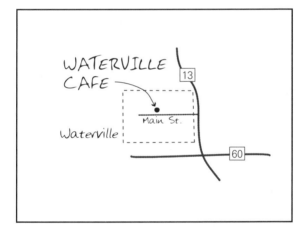

219 E. Main St., Waterville, MN 56096

Hours: Mon - Sat 6 a.m. - 8 p.m.
        Sun 6 a.m. - 2 p.m.
        Closed Easter and Christmas

Breakfast served to 11 a.m.

Smoking in designated area

Cash only

Phone: 507-362-8977

WHALEN

Overland Inn

Hidden in tiny Whalen, the Overland Inn is a Minnesota treasure. Though well known by sports enthusiasts on the Root River Trail, either by bike or canoe, the Inn requires a short hop from Minnesota 16 into Whalen.

The menu is small and simple. Homemade soups and sandwiches which by design reflect a healthy and outdoorsy structure, comprise the menu's luncheon selections.

It is the fresh oven-baked goods, however, that transform the Overland Inn into an extraordinary event. The world famous pies created daily in the kitchen include Cherry and Blueberry Decadence, raspberry pecan, and named for their authors, "Mayers" Maple Walnut and Chocolate "Addicks" Fudge.

If in the area, the Overland Inn merits a detour.

*The fresh oven-baked goods trans-
form the Overland Inn into an
extraordinary event.*

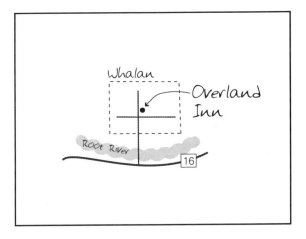

618 Main St., Whalen, MN 55949)
Hours: 1st weekend/May - 3rd weekend /Oct
             10 a.m. - 5 p.m. Daily
          Call ahead for other seasonal hours
No smoking
Cash only
Phone: 800-240-4162, 507-467-2623

Visiting the Twin Cities?

This section is a guide for visitors (and residents) who want to explore the unique dining character of the Twin Cities in just one, two or three days. The Yellow Pages list over 1,500 restaurants in the Twin Cities with over 900 in Minneapolis and over 600 in St. Paul. This does not include restaurants with multiple locations but may include some restaurants who choose to be listed in both places. In any case, the number is daunting when it comes time to choose a restaurant and being a visitor, you have little time and nothing to base your selection on other than advertisements.

We are making recommendations based on a traveling objective which Jerris (Mrs. Warner) and I employ in our travels - to discover restaurants with local flavor and clientele. The recommendations are based on personal experience and to an even larger degree the following: AUTHENTICY of foods (especially in ethnic categories), QUALITY, AMBIANCE (with credit for cleanliness of the neighborhood café ranking equally with the character of the more notable establishments), and finally UNIQUENESS of character (the real reason for choosing to use the guide's recommendations).

This visitor's guide is divided into two sections, one for Minneapolis and one for St. Paul. It radiates from both city centers so visitors staying near the International Airport will need transportation to the downtown areas. For those staying downtown, most eateries are within reasonable public transport. Where distances are greater, and therefore may be prohibitive for someone on a tight timeline, the restaurant is marked with and asterisk (*).

The descriptions are listed in the order in which they could be visited based on location. Many are interchangeable, however, such as Bryant Lake Bowl for breakfast and Victor's 1959 Café for lunch.

MINNEAPOLIS

If you have one day

Breakfast – Peter's Grill
Lunch – Gluek's
Dinner – Murray's

- OR -

Breakfast - Al's Breakfast
Lunch – Bryant Lake Bowl
Dinner – Murray's

If you have two days add

Breakfast - Victor's*
Lunch - Matt's Bar*
Dinner - Jax Cafe*

If you have two days add

Breakfast - du Jour's Casual Cafe
Lunch - Uptown Bar and Cafe
Dinner - Taco Morelos

ST. PAUL

If you have one day

Breakfast – Capitol View Cafe
Lunch – The Lexington
Dinner – W•A Frost and Company

If you have two days add

Breakfast – Day By Day Cafe
Lunch – Mildred Pierce Cafe
Dinner – Yarusso's

If you have two days add

Breakfast – Mickey's
Lunch – Mac's Fish & Chips
Dinner – Cherokee Sirloin Room

The above represent a reasonably conservative assembly of dining choices and ones which certainly satisfy the appetite. In addition to the above I have included a group of restaurants which deserve serious consideration as alternative selections. The reader will note some are farther afield than others though well within the metro area, while a few expand the palate by offering authentic ethnic cuisine. They are all marvelous experiences.

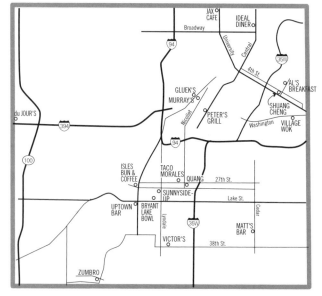

Minneapolis

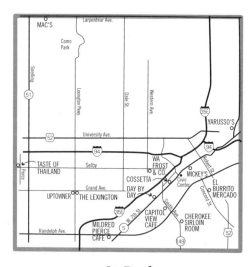

St. Paul

Minneapolis & St. Paul

MINNEAPOLIS

Al's Breakfast

No one should leave the planet without experiencing breakfast at Al's. Located in Dinkeytown on the "U's" campus, Al's is a bona fide institution!

This 14-stool, narrow (an understatement of classic proportions) little cafe has been serving breakfast for 50 years (anniversary date May 14, 1950) to seriously deranged and devoted fans who "will" themselves to stand in pouring rain, driving snow, blistering heat – or whatever, for the opportunity to sit on one of those famous stools and down a classic breakfast.

In measure the menu lists food categories of meats, eggs, flapjacks, waffles, fancy scrambled eggs, special omelettes and personal additions. The latter takes the egg grouping and supplies a host of add-ons with creations left to the boundless imagination.

Egg choices include benedict or poached on corned beef hash; flapjacks are served with walnuts, blueberries, white kernel corn, strawberries or blackberries. Spike, Leonard, Huevos Rancheros and the Israeli Special are among the fancy scrambled egg selections. Omelettes that are available are The Philip, The Smokey, New Orleans, Dinkytown and West Bank.

The atmosphere is created by instantaneous immersion.

No one should leave the planet without experiencing breakfast at Al's.

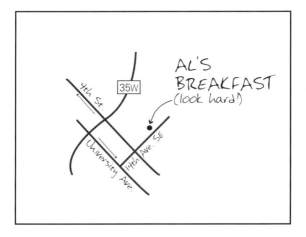

413-14th Ave. SE*, Mpls., MN 55414

Hours: Mon - Sat 6 a.m. - 1 p.m.
        Sun 9 a.m. - 1 p.m.
        Closed major Holidays

No smoking

Cash or check only

Phone: 612-331-9991

* Look for a little "hole-in-the-wall" on the West side of the Street

MINNEAPOLIS

Bryant Lake Bowl

Yes Virginia there is a bowling alley with a REAL restaurant on the premises – in fact, the primary reason to head for the Bryant Lake Bowl is the food, with bowling fashionable as either a social or party event. The BLB (as the cafe and its potatoes are known) is also adjacent to a Theatre of some notoriety, but that's also beside the point.

Though the Bryant Lake Bowl has been a restaurant since the 1950s, it's in the last few years with the creation of a new menu theme that the cafe has established its reputation. With the emphasis on freshness, entrees lean to fruit, veggies, granola, egg, and their famous BLB fries (fresh skin on chunks of small red potatoes with garnish). There are some special breakfast scrambles including broccoli, feta, peppers and spinach. Among the omlettes are a chili, Very Veggie and a Black Bean Plus.

The limited lunch and dinner selections (there seem to be more appetizers than entrees) include sandwiches and specialties. On the sandwich side the menu includes a Black Bean Burger, Peanut Noodle Wrap, Reuben, or a Cheddar and Guacamole. Among the specials are a Leek and Goat Cheese Frittata, Polenta, and a Penne with Lemon Cream Sauce. Note – the specials change weekly.

There is a very loyal following for the BLB with good reasons – atmosphere and food.

Try their famous BLB fries (fresh skin on chunks of small red potatoes with garnish).

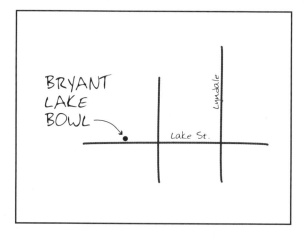

810 W. Lake St., Mpls., MN 55408
Hours: Daily 8 a.m. - 1 a.m.
        Closed Thanksgiving, Christmas Day
Breakfast served to 3:00 p.m. daily
Lunch served from 11:00 a.m.-5:00 p.m.
Dinner served from 5:00 p.m.-12:30 a.m.
Smoking in designated area
Credit cards accepted
Phone: 612-825-3737

MINNEAPOLIS (GOLDEN VALLEY)

du Jour's Casual Café

The du Jour's represents an exception to a general rule (and also a personal one) that office buildings fail to house restaurants of note or character.

The management and staff of du Jour's have created a menu of entrees with exceptional taste using nutritional balance, fresh ingredients and imagination.

The breakfast menu is extensive. Great choices include a Santa Fe or Sir Benedict Omelette, the Pheasants Banquet or Vagabond Skillet, biscuits and gravy, homespun griddle 'cakes, or signature dishes including a marvelous Green Fields Forever.

For lunch, du Jour's offers melts, salads, Iron Kettle Soup (not just a burger) and their special sandwiches such as The State Fair, Join The Club and Cajun Chick.

Though in the building's lower level the restaurant opens to the grounds behind, and using appealing decor with creative sectionalization, atmosphere is both cozy and private.

Given the restaurant's popularity and large following, a short wait may be expected.

The du Jour's represents an exception to a (personal) general rule that office buildings fail to house restaurants of note or character.

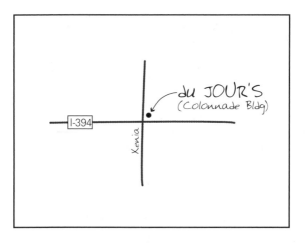

5500 Wayzata Blvd, Golden Valley, MN 55416
(Colonnade Bldg - NE corner of I-394 and Xenia)
Hours: Mon - Fri 6:30 a.m. - 2:30 p.m.
       Sat - Sun 7 a.m. - 2:30 p.m.
       Closed major Holidays
Breakfast served all day
Children's menu
Smoking in designated area
Credit cards accepted
Phone: 952-591-5033

MINNEAPOLIS

Gluek's

The atmosphere of this family-owned and operated restaurant is reason enough for a visit. In addition to having retreated into a sanctuary of wood, and a relaxed pace associated with years gone by, the food is superbly prepared and offers some wonderful ethnic choices.

The building in which Gluek's is located was first constructed by the family as a bar in 1902. Subsequent to a fire in 1989, the structure was completely restored to continue its unique addition to the downtown area.

Food selections begin with appetizers of Bratwurst Scallion Pot Stickers, Baked Brie and Baguette, or Reuben Egg Rolls. Sandwiches include the Berliner, Bismark (a brat baked on rye bread with sauerkraut, sour cream and Swiss cheese), Augustus Gloop, or fish and chips. Among the burger variations are a Can Am and the Black and Bleu.

Dinner selections include a choice of steak, walleye, pork chops, and the Bourbon Street Chicken, Wild Berry, Caesar and Haus salads are also on the menu. The all-you-can-eat New Orleans style fish fry attracts a crowd every Friday. The meal includes cajun catfish, hush puppies, red beans and rice as well as coleslaw. Blue Plate specials are available throughout the week.

The food is superbly prepared and offers some wonderful ethnic choices.

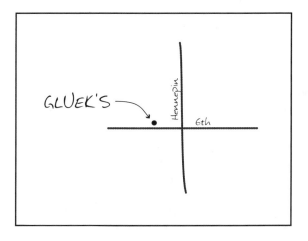

16 N. 6th St. (6th & Hennepin), Mpls., MN 55403

Hours: Food served Mon - Sat 11 a.m. - 11 p.m.
Full bar until 1 a.m.
Closed Sun

Smoking in designated area

Credit cards accepted

Phone: 612-338-6621

www.glueks.com

MINNEAPOLIS

Ideal Diner

The Ideal Diner has been a cafe for 50 years. For 32 of those years hostess Donna Stevens has been behind the counter bringing faith and care (not simply service) to her "family" on a daily basis, while owner (for the last 19 years) Kevin Kelzenberg is at the helm preparing those simply wonderful grilled foods.

This is a simple – albeit even a plain cafe, but in its own way that is its charm. It is what it is – a counter of 14 stools where you're closer to the stove than in your own kitchen. In fact it's not uncommon to simply tell Kevin when you'd like to add to your order, it's normally not more then 5 or 6 feet. The logo says it all.

The menu is eggs and meat (omelettes are excellent), hamburgers or sandwiches with a bowl of homemade soup or chili. No inventions here, just wonderful grill foods. Hash browns are fresh, frying along side the thick bacon (under the press – with maybe a sausage patty or two sitting atop just keeping warm) and the special pancakes grilling alongside. Kevin won't share the recipe except to say the batter contains "lot's of eggs," which judging from appearances no one's going to disagree.

The Ideal opens at 4:30 a.m. And as Donna relates she has her "guardians" waiting for her when she arrives to start the day's activities. Regulars, along with students from the "U," and the arriving families make the Ideal a tradition.

It is what it is - a counter of 14 stools where you're closer to the stove than in your own kitchen.

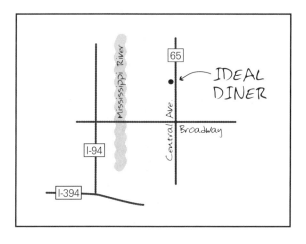

1314 Central Ave. NE, Mpls., MN 55413
Hours: Mon - Sat 4:30 a.m. - 2:00 p.m.
Sun 7 a.m. - 2 p.m.
Breakfast all day
Smoking in designated area
Cash only
Phone: 612-789-7630

MINNEAPOLIS

ISLES
BUN & COFFEE CO

Isles Bun & Coffee Co.

THE PLACE for cinnamon or caramel pecan rolls—most certainly in Minnesota and maybe the country! Honest to goodness, made-from-scratch, melt in your mouth, gooey, calorie laden, unbeatable buns.

The Isles even provides self-service, add-on frosting (their own special recipe), from a counter top container from which the devoted "lap" on these marvelous creations as the arteries chug away.

All the edibles (scones, muffins and fruit turnovers) are washed down with some of the best coffee in town – served up mild, medium or dark roasted.

There are other items to note. The Isles' lunches include a house specialty cheese toast with garlic powder, provolone cheese and tomatoes served with or without basil. Sandwiches, prepared on their freshly made buns consist of a choice between smoked ham and turkey, with toppings of Swiss, provolone, onions, tomatoes, sprouts or cucumbers.

Not much in the way of space so seating and standing room is limited. Weather permitting patrons use the Isle's sidewalk table and chairs to linger over the goodies.

Honest to goodness, made-from-scratch, melt in your mouth, gooey, calorie laden, unbeatable buns.

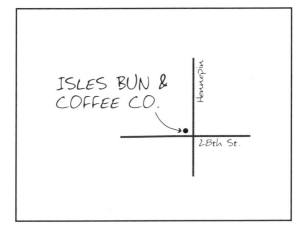

1422 W. 28th St., Mpls., MN 55408
Hours: Daily 6:30 a.m. - 5 p.m.
　　　　 Closed major Holidays
Cash or check only
Phone: 612-870-4466

MINNEAPOLIS

Jax Cafe

Odds are, anyone new to the Twin Cities inquiring of dinner ideas, will be pointed in the direction of Jax Cafe.

With the passing of venerated eating institutions, Jax remains one of a few recognized, renowned and respected restaurants. Family owned and operated since 1933, the Cafe has consistently offered the finest in food, service and ambiance. Smartly attired, the professional waitstaff assures the perfect dining experience.

Lunches include daily Iron Kettle creations. Beef stew on Monday, Swedish Meatballs on Wednesday and their most popular "kettle" chicken and dumplings on Thursday. Among the favorites cold salads available are a grilled chicken, shrimp and a variety of Caesars. The Lighter Side menu offers both cold and hot sandwiches, with selections from the Fish Market and Broiler available.

It would be difficult to pass over the steak entrees (prime rib, tournedos, strip to name a few), however Jax tempts the diner with ribs, lamb chops, chicken Kiev or Wellington, lobster and a variety of fish selections.

In season, the enchanting garden-patio is a unique and wonderful dining area including a stream where the guest may net their own trout.

With a tradition spanning several decades, Jax continues to personalize matchbooks for those sharing a special occasion. Simply be sure and advise the staff when making a reservation.

In season, the enchanting garden-patio is a unique and wonderful dining area including a stream where the guest may net their own trout.

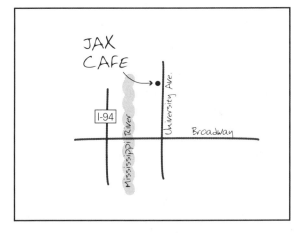

1928 University Ave. N.E., Mpls., MN*

Hours: Mon - Thurs 11 a.m. - 10 p.m.
    Fri - Sat 11 a.m. - 11 p.m.
    Sun 10 a.m. - 9 p.m. (Brunch 10 a.m. - 3 p.m.
      Last seating at 1:30 p.m.)

Children's menu

Smoking in designated area

Credit cards accepted

Phone: 612-789-7297

*Tending toward the formal

MINNEAPOLIS

Matt's Bar

THE BEST hamburgers in the Twin Cities. Based on awards from various sources, Matt's reputation is well deserved.

The grill's famous Jucy Lucy is the only burger known to come with a warning. Initial nibbles are to be taken with extreme caution. Failure to heed this advice results in an instantaneous searing of some very tender surfaces. This is due to the piping hot melted cheese encased between the two patties of the Lucy.

With patience the result is a trip to burger heaven. Below is Matt's menu – enjoy!

Hamburger

Cheeseburger

Double Hamburger with Cheese

Jucy Lucy

Grilled Cheese

Ham and Cheese

Ham and Rye

Chicken Sandwich

Turkey Sandwich

French Fries

½ order Fries

THE BEST hamburgers in the Twin Cities.

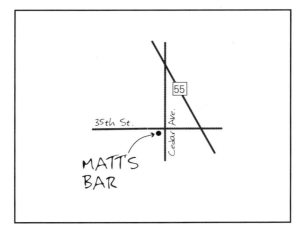

3500 Cedar Ave. S., Mpls., MN 55407

Hours: Mon - Wed 11 a.m. - 12 midnight
         Thurs - Sat 11 a.m. - 1 a.m.
         Sun 12 noon - 12 midnight
         Closed Holidays

Smoking in designated area

Cash or check only

Phone: 612-722-7072

MINNEAPOLIS

Murray's

Murray's

There are three things we can be sure of in our life-time – the other two are reasonably familiar, and if Murray's isn't it should be! This really is a Minnesota tradition and landmark. Everyone has to eat at Murray's, at least once.

The dinner menu is classic American cusine with the emphasis on steak. For the uninitiated, Murray's invented the term quality. House specialties include the Golden Butter Knife, Classic Porterhouse and Charteaubriand. Broiler choices include seven steak entrees, pork chops, veal t-bone, or rack of lamb. The preparation is exact and their meat selection processes have remained unchanged since 1933. Murray's own meat cutter hand-inspects the five tons of beef served monthly in the restaurant's dining room which assures the highest quality levels are maintained.

For customers who desire alternative entrees, there are fine fish and seafood, pasta, chicken breast and ostrich steak also available.

A complete complement of appetizer options are available to begin the meal with the dining experience enhanced by piano music beginning at 6:00 p.m. Thursday through Saturday and a violin added at 7:00 p.m.

The luncheon selections include a variety of sand-wiches, salads, combinations and entrees served with garlic toast, bakery rolls and a choice of salads and vegetables.

As expected, the dessert menu is also a list of rich wonderful creations.

This really is a Minnesota tradition (everyone has to eat at Murray's – at least once).

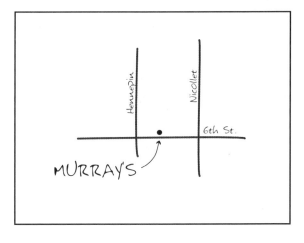

26 S. 6th St., Mpls., MN 55402*

Hours: Lunch: Mon - Fri 11 a.m. - 3 p.m.
           Dinner: Sun 4 p.m. - 10 p.m.
               Mon - Thurs 4 p.m. - 10:30 p.m.
               Fri - Sat 4 p.m. - 11 p.m.

Smoking is permitted in the Bar Area only

Credit cards accepted

Phone: 612-339-0909

*Tending toward the formal

MINNEAPOLIS

Peter's Grill

As the city's oldest cafe, its history dates to 1914 when it was initially established in downtown Minneapolis by founder Peter Atcas. Peter's has, over the years been a destination restaurant for a long list of celebrity figures, the latest of which was 1995, when President Bill Clinton stopped in for lunch.

Peter summed up his business theory in these words, "good homemade food, a lot of food and good prices." Current operators, nephews Andy and Peter Atsidakos continue these traditions.

There are 12 numbered breakfast offerings to anchor the menu, with omelettes and steak, ham, or Canadian bacon served with eggs as alternatives.

Among the the luncheon selections are Popular/wiches, 3 Decker/wiches and salads. Naturally burgers are a mainstay. Assorted diversions include a Reuben, Canadian bacon and eggs, gyro plate, or a fillet of whitefish.

The cafe also features steaks and chops broiled to order, fried spring chicken, beef liver (with bacon or onions), and seafoods of Walleye, whitefish, scallops, or shrimp. Their legendary Wednesday special (it's been on the menu for 25 years) is a $\frac{1}{4}$ Baked Spring Chicken with dressing, cabbage salad, fresh mashed potatoes, cranberry sauce and homemade roll at an unbeatable price. The dinner entrees include soup or juice, tossed or cabbage salad, choice of potato and homemade roll.

Not to be overlooked is their award winning Apple Pie!

The cities oldest cafe, its history dates to 1914.

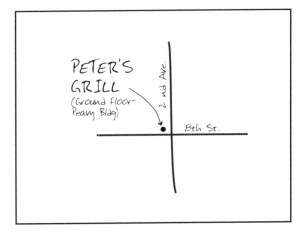

114 So. 8th St., Mpls., MN 55402
Hours: Mon - Fri 7 a.m. - 7:45 p.m.
        Sat 8 a.m. - 2:45 p.m.
        Closed Sun
        Call for Holiday Schedule
Breakfast served to 10:45 a.m.
Dinner service begins at 4 p.m.
Smoking in designated area
Credit cards accepted
Phone: 612-333-1981

MINNEAPOLIS

QUANG

Quang Restaurant

There are few ethnic restaurants in the Twin Cities which can be considered truly authentic and original. Quang has been mentioned as one of the top six restaurants in Minnesota by the New York Times. To experience the home-style cooking of Vietnam is to dine at the Quang.

The menu, written in both Vietnamese with English definitions is easily understood, with any questions readily answered by their friendly and knowledgeable staff.

Since its inception in 1989 the restaurant has grown in size and reputation. For authenticity and simply good food, Quang is the choice.

The menu features classic, simple Vietnamese dishes. Beginning with appetizers of Spring Rolls and Steamed Bun Dumpling, main entrees are then divided into Bun-Vermicelli Salads, platters and soups.

From the salad list (choices are served with rice-vermicelli), choices include stir-fried shrimp, stir-fried beef, grilled pork, or vegetarian stir-fried Tofu and mock duck. There are four platter dishes (served with Vietnamese fish sauce) and 15 varieties of soups. The latter are popular selections and range from beef stew and fish combinations, to meat balls.

Weekend specials are available Friday, Saturday and Sunday.

To experience the home-style cooking of Vietnam is to dine at the Quang.

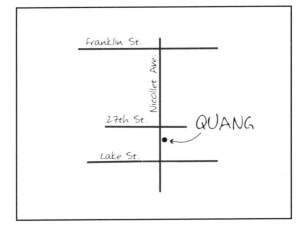

2719 Nicollet Ave. S, Mpls., MN 55408

Hours: Sun - Thurs 10 a.m. - 8:30 p.m.
        Fri - Sat 10 a.m. - 9 p.m.
        Closed Tues
        Open every Holiday

Smoking in designated area

Credit cards accepted

Phone: 612-870-4739

MINNEAPOLIS

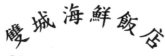

SHUANG CHENG
RESTAURANT

Shuang Cheng

A Dinkytown hot spot, Shuang Cheng has been crowding loyalists into their distinctive restaurant for the last 10 years. This is authentic Chinese cuisine with a typical menu of two zillion choices.

Hot steaming portions are served with abandon by a staff constantly in motion. Plates are piled high with an assortment of creations to rival anyone's imagination.

There are some very attractive Chef's suggestions, along with Szechuan specialties and hot pot, vegetarian, barbecue, chicken, beef, pork and seafood subgroups. Naturally, various types of noodles and rice preparations make an apppearance.

Shuang Cheng does feature Monday to Saturday daily lunch and Cantonese rice plate specials. With their substantial portions, it's common to observe those "little white containers" heading home for the fridge. For those with a bent toward the trivia, Shuang Cheng translates to "Twin City."

This is authentic Chinese cuisine with a typical menu of two zillion choices.

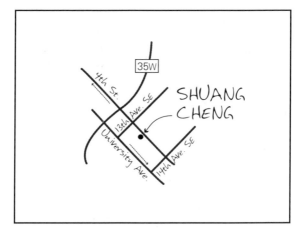

1320-4th St. SE, Mpls., MN 55414
Hours: Mon - Thurs 11 a.m. - 10 p.m.
   Fri - Sat 11 a.m. - 11 p.m.
   Sun 4 p.m. - 10 p.m.
Smoking in designated area
Credit cards accepted
Phone: 612-378-0208

MINNEAPOLIS

Sunnyside-Up Cafe

If you wonder why the customers routinely line up outside the Sunnyside Up Cafe on South Lyndale (in all kinds of weather) the reason is that the rations are served hot from a great grill.

The lively cafe is a bustle of motion. Their excellent waitstaff moves effortlessly taking orders, filling cups and carrying orders from the kitchen.

Though not identified as such on the menu, there are some house specialties which need to be sampled. The blue corn pancakes, prickly cactus or super plate of American fries are simply too good to pass up. Daily specials listed on the blackboard also deserve consideration.

Breakfast selections include egg combos, omlettes (choice of ingredients), Mexican breakfast specialties and pancake combinations. Monday to Friday features nicely priced breakfast entrees.

Lunch is served Monday to Friday only and includes sandwiches (a great clubhouse), burgers and salads.

The blue corn pancakes, prickly cactus or super plate of American fries are simply too good to pass up.

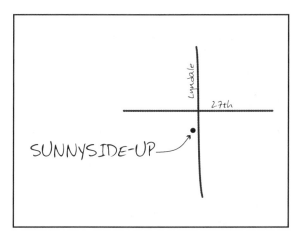

2704 Lyndale Ave. S, Mpls., MN 55408
Hours: Mon - Fri 6:30 a.m. - 3 p.m.
        Sat - Sun 7 a.m. - 3 p.m.
        Closed major Holidays
Breakfast served all day
Children's menu
Smoking in designated area
Cash or check only
Phone: 612-870-4817

MINNEAPOLIS

**AUTHENTIC FRESH
MEXICAN COOKING**

Taco Morelos

A lot of restaurants lay claim to serving real Mexican foods – the fact that Taco Morelos actually lives up to the promise sets it apart from the rest.

In just over four years, this nondescript little cafe has established itself as a Twin Cities Best.

Breakfasts begin with the familiar Huevos Rancheros, with menu add-ons like Huevos en Salsa Verde and Huevos con Chorizo. These are served with a choice of two side dishes of either Mexican-style potatoes, rice or beans.

After breakfast there are a number of appetizers (13) which lead to soups and assorted entrees.

Main course choices are imposing and impressive. Fish (orange roughy, red snapper and shrimp), beef (including steaks) and pork are all prepared to authentic Mexican recipes.

Customary Mexican fare with the Taco Morelos touch of some wonderful specialties include tacos, burritos, fajitas and enchiladas.

Vegetarian dishes are available in most of the entrée categories.

Customary Mexican fare with the Taco Morelos touch of some wonderful specialties.

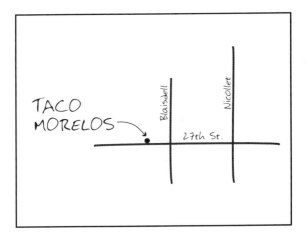

14 W. 26th St., Mpls., MN 55404

Hours: Mon - Thurs 9 a.m. - 10 p.m.
       Fri - Sat 9 a.m. - 2 p.m.
       Sun 9 a.m. - 12 noon
       Closed major Holidays

Breakfast served all day

No smoking

Credit cards accepted

Phone: 612-870-0053

MINNEAPOLIS

Uptown Bar and Cafe

Since the 1930s the Uptown has been a cafe, and a quick study of the menu cements it as a dynamic restaurant. The six pages of choices represent an abundance of entrees and a wide selection of basics.

Starting with a famed caramel roll (this is a biggie), the man-sized breakfasts are rolled out in the form of skillets (piled high), omelettes (formidable) and egg-meat variations. Pancakes, waffles and French toast are also on the menu.

Lunch and dinner begin with a medley of appetizers including nachos, dips, a baked brie or onion burst.

Fresh salads, burgers, pitas, hot sandwiches, the sandwich boar, and soup specials are lunchtime features. Platters, the Poulet, gyro hash, beef hash and favorites including a buffalo chicken breast, tuna steak sandwich and a beef dip are also mainstays for the regulars. Another Uptown favorite is their Roast Turkey which is available as either a sandwich or dinner. Among the dinner items (which include a choice of soup, salad or coleslaw accompanied by country-style bread) are homemade meatloaf, liver and onions or roast beef.

Bring an appetite!

Starting with a famed caramel roll (a biggie), the man-sized breakfasts are rolled out in the form of skillets, omelettes and egg-meat variations.

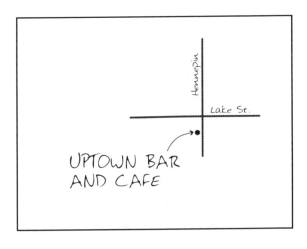

3018 Hennepin Ave. S, Mpls., MN 55408
Hours: Summer 8 a.m. - 11 p.m.
        Winter 8 a.m. - 10 p.m.
        Closed Christmas Day
Breakfast all day
Patio dining available (weather permitting)
Smoking in designated area
Cash or check only
Phone: 612-823-4719

MINNEAPOLIS

Victor's 1959 Café

Thankfully, Victor Valens has chosen Minneapolis to set up shop and thus added a new and unique dimension to the dining scene. Where else can we order Yuca and Eggs or Eggs Havana. The latter exposes Victor's culinary theme which brings a little of Cuba to the Twin Cities.

The above entrees plus Ranchero Cubano and the Black Bean Scrambler are the primary ethnic breakfast choices along with traditional American fares. Featuring some of the best biscuits and gravy in the state, the little diner also prepares excellent pancakes and offers a create-your-own omelette option.

Lunch, served after 11 a.m., includes a Cuban and a Cuban steak sandwich plus burgers, served with a choice of French fries or plantain chips.

Note, Victor does plan additional Cuban entrees for the menu later this year.

The atmosphere of the 1950s converted-gas-station resembles crowded confusion with just the right splash of color and "ricketyness" to create a neat dining experience.

*Where else can we order Yuca and
Eggs or Eggs Havana.*

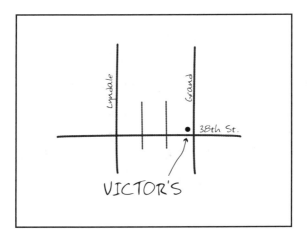

3756 Grand Ave. S., Mpls., MN 55409
Hours: Tues - Fri 6:30 a.m. - 2:30 p.m.
        Sat 7:30 a.m. - 2:30 p.m.
        Sun 8 a.m. - 2 p.m.
        Closed Mondays and major Holidays
Breakfast all day
No Smoking
Cash or check only
Phone: 612-827-8948
E-mail: cafe1959@aol.com

MINNEAPOLIS

Village Wok

This busy, popular University of Minnesota campus Chinese dining hall specializes in seafood of all kinds and descriptions. Adding to those entrees are their daily specials, which you have to look for on sheets of paper taped to the walls. Altogether there are an astounding 339 distinctive creations divided into various subgroups.

The Wok has all the expectations of an eatery true to its origins. Fried rice, chop suey, sweet and sour and lo mein all find their way on the menu.

Among the Szechuan cuisine specialties are entrees of beef, pork and vegetables. Cantonese features include walleye, trout, sole, salmon, lobster, squid, scallops and shrimp. On the meat side duck, chicken and pork find their way to the score sheet along with vegetarian and noodle dishes.

This is a busy-busy restaurant filled with students, professors and devoted customers who love the food, service and price.

This is a busy-busy restaurant filled with students, professors and devoted customers who love the food, service and price.

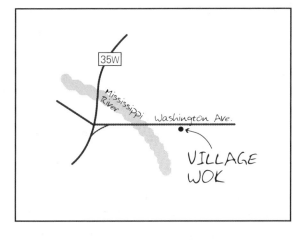

610 Washington Ave. SE, Mpls , MN 55414

Hours: 11 a.m. - 1:40 a.m. Daily
        Closed - July 4th, Thanksgiving Day,
        Christmas Day

Smoking in designated area

Credit cards accepted

Phone: 612-331-9041

MINNEAPOLIS

Zumbro

Located in an area of quaint shops in south Minneapolis and within easy walking distance to Lake Harriet, Zumbro is a standout cafe.

Not to be dispirited by their theme of "unconventional dishes served daily," their strength lies in using the freshest of foods and ingredients to prepare creative (but not threatening) entrees.

Chef Neil Holman, who received his training in California, brings a touch to edibles seldom found in Minnesota. Safe to say, the Zumbro is not for devotees of the beef commercial (bread, meat, mashed potatoes, gravy) or lutefisk.

The crowds, and they are many, arrive in droves for homemade buttermilk and buckwheat wild rice pancakes or French toast prepared with Italian striato bread. From the menu's "sides" segment, do not miss the Roasted Rosemary Potatoes. Fresh fruit, Zumbro oatmeal, or special homemade granola (aka Zumbrola) are great starters.

With egg dishes, the restaurant features daily specials as well as menu entrees of Spinach Eggs or Huevos Zumbrosos.

Lunches preserve the Zumbro's theme. Refreshing, palate pleasing ideas include ziti with broccoli and sun-dried tomatoes, Penne with grilled chicken or grilled tuna with organic greens. Delightful soup specials are a daily feature and may include squash, corn chowder, tomato-potato basil or a chicken tortilla.

The atmosphere is open, crowded and contempory.

The truth lies in using the freshest of foods and ingredients to prepare creative (but not threatening) entrees.

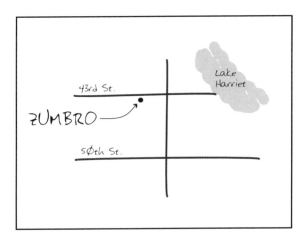

2803 W. 43rd St., Mpls., MN 55410
Hours: Tues - Fri 7 a.m. - 2:30 p.m.
            Sat - Sun 7:30 a.m. - 2:30 p.m.
            Closed Mon and major Holidays
Breakfast served to 11:30 a.m. Tues - Sat, all day Sun
No smoking
Credit cards accepted
Phone: 612-920-3606

ST. PAUL

CAPITOL VIEW
CAFE

Capitol View Cafe

For 15 years the Capitol View has been on Smith Street as it runs up the hill from downtown St. Paul. From this location, the optimum view of the Capitol building is from the middle of the street – and depending on traffic, can be a pretty picture.

Sort of a Mexican, Tex-Mex, American collage of entrees, the Capitol View prepares a mix of choices. In some ways this reflects the atmosphere which resembles a "hither and thither" collection of crowded dining areas attended to by a busy waitstaff.

Breakfasts offer a selection of 'cakes including blueberry and banana pecan or buttermilk and Belgian waffles. There is an agreeably priced Capitol View Special, biscuits and gravy, and assorted house specialties such as a cajun benedict, breakfast burrito and chorizo con huevos. Omelette choices include fajita, vegetarian and farmers.

Lunches start with a variety of appetizers such as Nachos Supreme, a list of main course salads (Chinese Chicken, Taco), homemade soups including a cajun chili, sandwiches (burgers, grilled tuna, patty melt and a BLT among the choices) and Mexican specials (tacos, tostados, combo platters).

Ice cream, malts, sundaes, pies and cakes are on the dessert menu.

*Sort of a Mexican, Tex-Mex, American
collage of entrees, the Capitol View
prepares a mix of choices.*

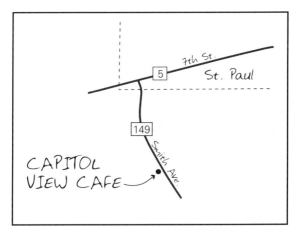

637 Smith St., St. Paul, MN 55107
Hours: Tues - Wed 7 a.m. - 3 p.m.
           Thurs - Sun 7 a.m. - 9 p.m.
           Closed Mon - Call for Holiday schedule
Breakfast served all day
Smoking in designated area
Credit cards accepted
Phone: 651-290-0218

ST. PAUL

Cherokee Sirloin Room

A family tradition which began in 1970 when Bob and Dorothy Casper purchased the Cherokee cafe (a bar and restaurant since 1934), the eatery is now operated by sons Rick and Jim Casper. Even though the restaurant has continued to expand, (the latest addition being 1998) Rick and Jim have continued to be guided by the principles of quality, value and service which have been the cornerstones of their success.

The Cherokee stresses its appeal as a family restaurant and matches a comprehensive children's menu with award-winning entrees.

Lunches feature house specialties including meat loaf, Minnesota Chicken Breast and Grandma Brotzler's Chicken Pot Pie. Naturally, steaks (handpicked and aged), along with beef stroganoff, BBQ pork ribs, burgers, or fish and seafood.

The evening menu provides a wide variety of dinner options. Entrée salads, favorite pastas, steaks and chops, ribs and chicken, fish and seafood, a Great Values section and burgers will accommodate everyone's appetite.

Atmosphere is that of a relaxed supper club with a predominately red-and-white color theme. As the customers expect, service is provided by their experienced staff, who carry out duties professionally and attentively.

Lunch specialties include Meat Loaf,
Minnesota Chicken Breast and
Grandma Brotzler s Chicken Pot Pie.

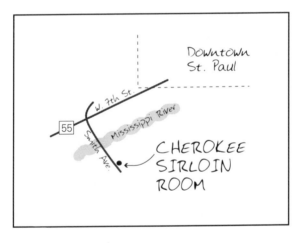

886 S. Smith Ave., W. St. Paul, MN 55118
Hours: Mon - Sat 11 a.m. - 10 p.m.
        Sun 10 a.m. - 9 p.m.
        (Brunch 10 a.m. - 2 p.m.)
        Closed major Holidays
Children's menu
Smoking in designated area
Credit cards accepted
Phone: 651-457-2729

* Can be formal upon occasion

ST. PAUL

Cossetta Italian Market & Pizzeria

There is only one Cossetta's – and only one restaurant like Cossetta's.

This busy eatery serves basic Italian fare, cafeteria-style, to the delight of a contingency of loyal patrons. Good fun, terrific tasteful foods and a unique charm result in a truly special experience.

Customers begin service by joining a line which may wander to either the back of the cafe or to the deli/grocery. Shoppers weave in and out with small bushel baskets used in acquiring a variety of fresh breads, pastas of every conceivable shape, size and description, homemade sauces, and cheeses or meats from the extensive butcher's counter.

Cossetta's has been around since 1911, first as a grocery store in St Paul's Italian neighborhood (there were some take out sandwiches and always their own recipe for sausage), then moving to West 7th street in 1984 and the opening of a pizza parlor. In 1988 the family established their present day market and stylish restaurant.

In the cafeteria, entrees include lasagna, veal parmigiano, chicken cacciatori, or sausage and peppers served with mostaccioli and garlic bread. Fresh salads and heros (hot or cold) are also on the chalkboard menu.

Famous for its authentic Italian pizza, the marvelous pies are ordered by the slice for service in the restaurant or are certainly available for take out.

Customers begin service by joining a line which may wander to either the back of the cafe or to the deli/grocery.

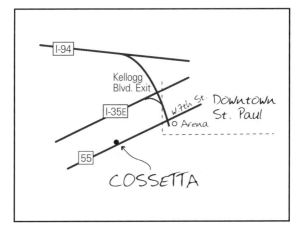

211 W. 7th St., St. Paul, MN 55102

Hours: Summer (May - Sept)
          Daily 11 a.m. - 9 p.m.
      Winter (Oct. - April)
          Mon - Thurs 11 a.m. - 9 p.m.
      Fri - Sat 11 a.m. - 10 p.m.
          Sun 11 a.m. - 8 p.m.
      Closed Major Holidays

No Smoking

Credit cards accepted

Phone: 651-222-3476

ST. PAUL

Day By Day Cafe

Day By Day Cafe

Setting for the Day By Day is reminiscent of the 60s in 'Frisco. With their creative menus, furnishings best described as miscellaneous, a cast of characters with a mission of Peace and Love, and a hodge podge of assorted books and "stuff," the kitchen provides the best in the way of cafe foods.

The use of some wonderful breads to accompany their breakfast choices is a great start. In addition to the basics, the cafe's scrambled eggs with cream cheese or spinach, granola with yogurt and fresh fruit, or the tofu-veggie scramble make some nice diversions. Homemade buttermilk and buckwheat pancakes are a house speciality.

At lunchtime, the Day By Day's menu moves to sandwiches, homemade soups and chili. The restaurant also prepares some noted salads including vegetarian, spinach and grilled chicken. Burger choices, available for lunch and dinner, include a salsa, guacamole and a mushroom. Among the dinner entrees are pork, chicken, beef, stir-fry and steamed vegetables with brown rice.

*Setting for the Day By Day is
reminiscent of the 60s in 'Frisco.*

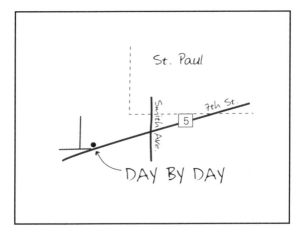

477 W. 7th St., St. Paul, MN 55102

Hours: Mon - Fri 6 a.m. - 8 p.m.
        Sat 6 a.m. - 3 p.m., Sun 7 a.m. - 3 p.m.
        Closed major Holidays

Breakfast served all day

No smoking

Cash or check only

Phone: 651-227-0654

ST. PAUL

El Burrito Mercado

Irrefutably Mexico without the air fare. This thriving little cafe forms a segment of a bustling cosmopolitan in-house community comprised of the best Mexican grocery store in the Twin Cities and a few arts and crafts.

Of particular interest are the displayed awards and the photograph of co-owner Maria Silva with former President Ronald Reagan.

The fresh foods are ordered cafeteria style and carried to one of several tables adjacent to the store separated by an iron railing.

Open for lunch or dinner, the posted menu features platters and individual dishes. From a simple selection patrons choose between platters of Polo ala Mexicana, Carnitas, and Birria, or tacos, tamales, tortas and quesadillas. This is the real thing!

The fresh foods are ordered cafeteria style and carried to one of several tables adjacent to the store separated by an iron railing.

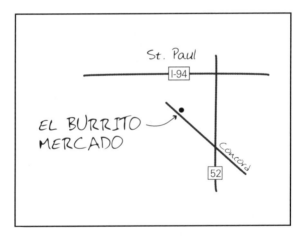

175 Concord St., St. Paul, MN 55107
Hours: Daily 8 a.m. - 6 p.m.
No smoking
Phone: 651-227-2192

ST. PAUL

The Lexington

The Lexington is St. Paul. For most of the city's residents it seems like the restaurant has been at the corner of Grand and Lexington forever, though it has only been since 1935.

Rumor has it that this site has produced more "deals" (both business and political) than any other place in the city – and maybe the state.

Among the Lexington's attractions are the legendary food and dining ambiance. Holding court is perfectly appropriate in either the wonderful formal dining room or the classic, darkly wooded bar area.

The menu is tried and true. At the heart of luncheon selections are marvelous salads, followed by a list of traditional favorites – lamb shanks and pot roast, joined by Chicken Tchoupitoulas or Chicken Vesuvio. Soup of the day is flavor filled and their Friday New England Clam Chowder is the best in the cities. Luncheon selections also include winning sandwiches and express items.

Dinners begin with wonderful appetizers, such as the Lexington's crab cakes, portabella mushrooms and coconut shrimp. Salad entrees include a Chicago Chop, Marine and Chicken Caesar.

The restaurant features "classic steaks and fresh seafood." Accompanying the main course is a choice between baked or mashed potatoes, followed by either homemade soup or salad with freshly baked bread. The menu also includes blackened pork chops, braised short ribs, and spring lamb chops.

The Lexington's attractions are the legendary food and dining ambiance.

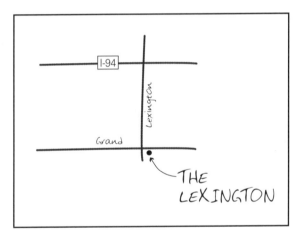

1096 Grand Ave., St. Paul, MN 55105
Hours: Mon - Thurs 11 a.m. - 10 p.m.
　　　　Fri - Sat 11 a.m. - 11 p.m.
　　　　Sun 10 a.m. - 9 p.m.
Smoking permitted in the Bar Area
Credit cards accepted
Phone: 651-222-5878

ST. PAUL

Mac's Fish & Chips

Except for the addition of chicken strips, the name describes the menu. Just maybe, what the Juicy Lucy is to the hamburger (see Matt's Bar in Minneapolis), deep fried halibut at Mac's is to fish.

The made over former gas station (don't count on ambiance), now Mac's home, serves up fish, chips and chicken strips (and a side of cole slaw) in a price per piece configuration with the cost reduced in proportion to the amount ordered. There is also a basket combo of fish and chicken served with the skin-on fries representing the extent of available options.

For the purist, save the adding of malt vinegar, the wonderful deep fried halibut is unbeatable. Evidence of the little shop's popularity is the return, and return, and return of their loyal and satisfied customers.

What the Juicy Lucy is to the hamburger, deep fried halibut at Mac's is to fish.

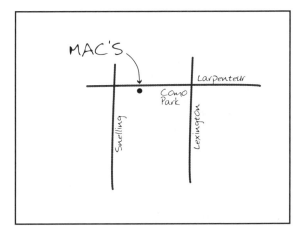

1330 Larpenteur Ave. W., St. Paul, MN 55113
Hours: Tues - Thurs, Sat 11 a.m. - 8:30 p.m.
        Fri 11 a.m. - 9 p.m.
        Closed Sun and Mon
No smoking
Cash or check
Phone: 651-489-5299

ST. PAUL

Mickey's

East coaster's are reasonably familiar with the concept of a roadside diner. In Minnesota, however, there is only one REAL diner. That is Mickey's. Transported to St. Paul by flatcar in 1934 from its New Jersey manufacturer, and now on The Register of National Historic Places, Mickey's has been at the same downtown location ever since.

Joining the ranks of celebrities (Rosanne, Arnold Schwartzenegger, Willard Scott, Garrison Keilor, and so forth) who have ventured into the confines of Mickey's, customers sit down to basic grill type foods.

Breakfasts include homemade buttermilk 'cakes, a southern pecan waffle, omlettes, steak or pork chop with eggs and those great homemade hash browns. Potatoes O'Brien are a house specialty.

Sandwiches, beyond the required burgers, include a menu of melts, Mickey's Sputnick, the Big Eric and a One-Eyed Jack. Homemade Mulligan stew and chili are always available. Dinners, with a choice of soup or salad, potatoes or baked beans include southern fried chicken, hamburger steak, liver and onions, or a fish filet.

As for character, realizing you're sitting in a classic is sufficient.

Transported to St. Paul by flatcar in 1934, now on the Register of National Historic Places.

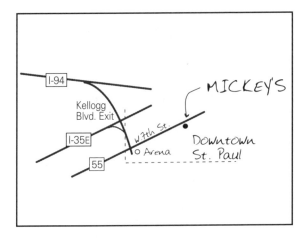

36 W. 7th St. (P.O. Box 16368), St. Paul, MN 55102
Hours: 24 hours Daily
Breakfast all day
Smoking in designated area
Phone: 651-698-0259

ST. PAUL

Mildred Pierce Cafe

Aficionados of the silver screen will recognize Mildred Pierce. For everyone else, the menu kindly explains the 1945 movie role played by Joan Crawford. Owner Shelagh Connolly named her restaurant in honor of the character whose spirit and determination and culinary skills resulted in a chain of restaurants.

The Cafe is a refreshing addition to the St. Paul scene. Foods are served in a comfortable dining area using a black-and-white color scheme with brightly hued wall accents.

Shelagh describes the entrees as traditional yet contemporary American foods. True to the mission, her variations on the basics are subtle but important. Eggs Benedict for example, include savory Spanish ham and a chipolte hollandaise sauce, and the luncheon BLT is made with applewood smoked bacon and white truffle aioli on wheat toast.

Breakfast, lunch and dinner selections concentrate on freshly prepared basics. Hash, omelettes, pancakes (with bananas and pecans or blueberries), waffles (assorted accessories on hand), eggs with a variety of meat options comprise breakfast, with salads and sandwiches for lunch. Soups, homemade and a cafe special are served at both lunch and dinner. Samples of daily soup specials include Green Apple Puree, split pea, tomato and white bean.

Dinners always feature a fresh fish, chicken, pork, beef and a pasta entrée. With a changing menu, which highlights the kitchens creativity and purpose, customers enjoy a fine variety of foods.

*The menu kindly explains the 1945
movie role played by Joan Crawford.*

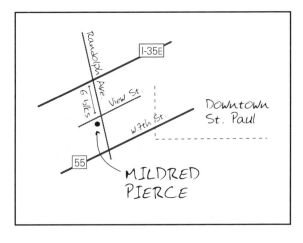

786 Randoph Ave., St. Paul, MN 55102
Hours: Tues - Thurs 7 a.m. - 9 p.m.
       Fri 7 a.m. - 10 p.m.
       Sat 8 a.m. - 10 p.m.
       Sun 8 a.m. - 1:30 p.m.
Breakfast served to 10:45 a.m. Tues - Fri
       1:30 p.m. Sat, Sun
Lunch is served Tues - Fri 11:15 a.m. - 2 p.m.
No smoking
Credit cards accepted
Phone: 651-222-7430

ST. PAUL

Taste Of Thailand

Taste Of Thailand

Not a question as to what to expect on your plate at the Taste Of Thailand. The challenging menu requires reflection on a wide variety of authentic ethnic creations.

Thai from start to finish, offerings begin with 23 assorted appetizers ranging from egg and spring rolls, to creamcheese puffs, deep-fried bananas or fried tofu, while beverages include cold and hot Thai tea, Thai lemonade and iced Thai coffee, with Thai custard at the finish line.

A variety of soups and salads are punctuated by egg drop, wonton and a nice stuffed cucumber.

The major entrees include curries, Pad Thai, Rad Na, Pad Pak and Pad Prig Khing. Choices of ingredients include vegetarian, beef, chicken, pork and shrimp. Foods are seasoned to taste and are ordered mild to hot. In Thai terms, hot is hot – and the advice is to be prepared accordingly.

During the week the restaurant features a small but adequate all-you-can-eat buffet.

The dwelling is a converted store with no real attempt at atmosphere. Customers arrive in crowds for the creations of the kitchen rather than the ambiance.

Thai from start to finish, offerings begin with 23 assorted appetizers ranging from egg and spring rolls, to cream cheese puffs, deep-fried bananas or fried tofu.

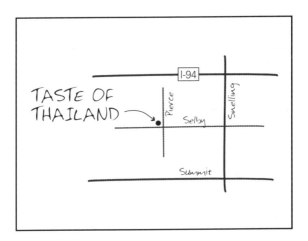

1671 Selby, St. Paul, MN 55104

Hours: Mon - Thurs 11 a.m. - 9 p.m.
           Fri - Sat 11 a.m. - 10 p.m.
           Sun 12 Noon - 8 p.m.
           Closed major Holidays

No smoking

Credit cards accepted

Phone: 651-644-3997

ST. PAUL

Uptowner On Grand

"Basic hash house" may be the best description for this popular eatery. A winning grill it produces (in edible form) 1800 eggs and 800 pounds of potatoes a week. The basics are transformed into some of the best breakfasts around.

The Uptowner specialties include a great cajun breakfast (also available with their special order cajun sausage), hash, Tex-Mex, farmers and eggs Benedict. Half orders are available and might be advisable for the less than greedy appetite. Combinations, a design-your-own-omlette, home-made buttermilk pancakes and waffles, or Texas-sized French toast round out the breakfast menu. The Uptowner's Early Bird Special is served Monday to Friday from 6:30 a.m. to 8:30 a.m. and includes eggs and toast with bacon or sausage. Hash browns are homemade from fresh potatoes.

Speciality sandwiches on the lunch board include a tuna-melt, Uptowner Club, French dip and a grilled Reuben or Rachael all served with French fries. Burgers come with a choice of fries or a cup of homemade soup or Uptowner chili.

Atmosphere is a utilitarian usage of booths, tables and counter space.

Basic hash house may be the best description for this popular eatery.

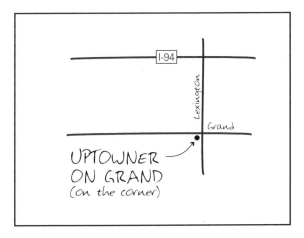

1100 Grand Ave., St. Paul, MN 55105

Hours: Daily Mon - Sat 6:30 a.m. - 3 p.m.
Sun 8 a.m. - 3 p.m.
Late night hours Thurs - Sat 10 p.m.- 3 a.m.

Breakfast served all day

Children's menu

Smoking in designated area

Cash or check only

Phone: 651-224-6418

ST. PAUL

W·A Frost and Company

Enter the romance of Camelot. By all accounts the ambiance of St. Paul's Frost and Company is unequaled in the Twin Cities. Set in the confines of the Dakotah Building's 1889 architecture the restaurant opened as a small cafe and bar in 1975. Evolution and addition, the first in 1977, has only added to the restaurant's charm and appeal. Diners are immersed in greenery, original and ornate oil paintings, oriental rugs and candlelight with a background of fireplaces, brick and timber. In season, customers flock to the wonderful garden patio.

It's reputation also extends to the kitchen which prepares a number of winning dishes.

For lunch Frost offers appetizers including home baked Focaccia, fried polenta, and homemade soups followed by main course entrees, salads and sandwiches.

Grilled trout, grilled pork T-bone, and Pot au Feu are among the entrees while roast beef, grilled salmon and a grilled Portobello mushroom are on the sandwich list.

For dinner Frost expands the starters menu, adds a nice selection of entree salads and introduces Magret of Duck, a Mixed Grill, Pan Roasted Sea Bass and Pasta e Fagioli as main courses.

W·A Frost is the perfect choice for special occasion dining offering atmosphere, service and food of distinction.

Enter the romance of Camelot.

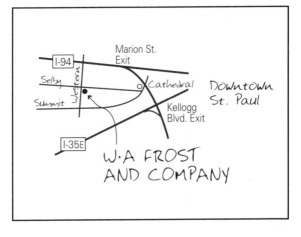

374 Selby (and Western Ave.), St. Paul, MN 55102
Hours: Mon - Sat 11 a.m. - 12 midnight
        Sun 10:30 a.m. - 11 p.m.
        (Brunch 10:30 a.m. - 2 p.m.)
        Closed major Holidays
Smoking in bar area only (food service provided)
Credit cards accepted
Phone: 651-224-5715

ST. PAUL

Yarusso's

Yarusso's has been a family tradition for 67 years.
The restaurant began when Francesco Yarusso
started the Square Deal Cafe in 1932 and changed
the name to Yarusso's. The restaurant is a haven
for loyalists attracting a large following for their
home cooked food using the same sauce recipe
Francesco created over 60 years ago.

Forget the fancy innovative dishes others use to
simulate Italian cooking. Yarusso's serves only real,
honest Italian family fare which continues to be so
popular in the small villages of their homeland.

The reason for the popularity of St. Paul's oldest
family-owned restaurant is the simple menu.
Devoted to pasta (spaghetti, mostaccioli, rigatoni
and ravioli) served with meatballs or sausage, and
entrees of chicken, meatballs, steak or fish, the
food is both basic and authentic. Their specials
vary daily, starting with lasagna on Monday to
Italian baked catfish on Friday and all-you-can-eat
spaghetti on Sunday.

Lunch specials (served from 11 a.m. to 4:30 p.m.),
salads, pizza and appetizers complete the menu.
The decor and charm carries through to the red-
and-white color scheme and crowded dining area.

Attracts a large following for their home cooked food using the same sauce recipe Francesco created some 60 years ago.

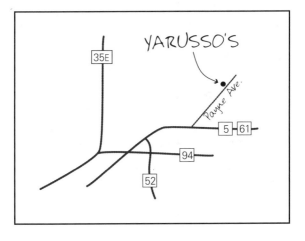

637 Payne Ave., St. Paul, MN 55101
Hours: 10 a.m. - 10 p.m. Daily
            Closed Easter, Thanksgiving, Christmas
Smoking in designated area
Credit cards accepted
Phone: 651-776-4848

About the Author

George and his wife Jerris consider themselves ardent travelers. With wisdom acquired by both success and failure they readily admit to a "bent" for searching and learning the real character of the lands and peoples in their journeys.

Jerris, with a background in theatre, and a B.S.E. degree, takes the role of explorer very seriously. Appropriate to species and gender (as well as most marriages) she is more likely to ask the questions resulting in the discovery of "off the beaten track" wonderful little hotels and eateries. This is of course accomplished with the slightest of winks, a small nod and a coquettish glance in the direction of her partner. Interestingly, this occurs, by some miracle or another, absent any indication whatso-ever of "I told you so."

George, whose background is business, has a Juris Doctorate degree from the University of Iowa. As a self proclaimed Minnesotan, he requests neither region nor profession be held against him.

The experiences of domestic and international travel, by these partners, provides the background to appropriately and objectively evaluate the quali-ty, character and service of these unique eateries.

The "youngish" grandparents, with looks and vigor that bespeak their ages, eagerly await the opportunity to explore the homestyle fare with the newest family additions.

Byway Eateries Feedback Form

Your feedback helps us improve this guidebook for future traveler. Please fill this out with your personal favorites and discoveries.

Number of customers in your party _____.

Ages of customers (including children)_____.

We recommend the following restaurants for inclusion in this guide:

Town_____

_____

Cafe/Restaurant_____

_____

Directions (if necessary)

_____

_____

_____

Of the restaurants included in this guide, which ones were:

Best: _____

_____

Why _____

_____

Worst: _____

_____

Why:_____

_____

How might this guide be improved: _____

_____

Optional:

Name _____

Street Address_____

City, State, Zip Code _____

Please return to:

George Warner
Adventure Publications
P.O. Box 269
Cambridge, MN 55008

City Index

Restaurant Index